Religious Studies (AS Philosophy)

Revisio

Brian Poxon

Published by Inducit Learning Ltd trading as pushmepress.com,

Pawlett House, West Street, Somerton,

Somerset TA11 7PS, United Kingdom

www.pushmepress.com

First published in 2012

ISBN: 978-1-909618-08-4

Links, reviews, news and revision materials available on

www.philosophicalinvestigations.co.uk

With over 20,000 visitors a month, the philosophical investigations website allows students and teachers to explore Philosophy of Religion and Ethics through handouts, film clips, presentations, case studies, extracts, games and academic articles.

Pitched just right, and so much more than a text book, here is a place to engage with critical reflection whatever your level. Marked student essays are also posted.

Contents

'The unexamined life is not worth living' Socrates

Introduction to Philosophy of Religion

GREEK INFLUENCES ON THE PHILOSOPHY OF RELIGION

METAPHYSICS explores the fundamental nature of existence and asks questions such as, what is meant by 'reality'? Is the physical world all that there is, or does ultimate reality lie elsewhere?

Understanding **PLATO**'s **ANALOGY OF THE CAVE** and his theory of the **REALM OF THE FORMS**. How does Plato argue for two 'worlds', one of unchanging knowledge and reality (the Forms), and one of illusion and opinion (the cave/shadow world)? Does his argument work?

Understanding **ARISTOTLE**'s ideas about **CAUSE** and **PURPOSE** and how this relates to God, known as the **PRIME MOVER**. What does Aristotle mean by the **FOUR CAUSES**, and **'POTENTIAL'** and **'ACTUAL'** in his approach to metaphysics? What does he mean by the idea of a Prime Mover?

JUDEAO-CHRISTIAN INFLUENCES ON THE PHILOSOPHY OF RELIGION

How do Greek ideas both influence, and differ from, **JUDAEO-CHRISTIAN** understandings of God?

Within the Judaeo-Christian tradition as outlined in the Bible, what is understood by the idea of God as **CREATOR** and God **CREATING FROM NOTHING** (Latin ex nihilo)? How is this idea different to Aristotle's **PRIME MOVER**? What do terms such as **OMNIPOTENCE**,

OMNISCIENCE and **OMNIPRESENCE** mean within the Judaeo-Christian tradition?

How is God understood to be **GOOD** within the Judaeo-Christian tradition, and what implications does this have for the idea of God as the source of ethics and law? What is the **DIVINE COMMAND THEORY** of ethics and its strengths and weaknesses?

TRADITIONAL ARGUMENTS FOR THE EXISTENCE OF GOD AND CHALLENGES TO THEM

An **A PRIORI** argument is something true by definition, from reason and before (prior to) empirical evidence.

The **ONTOLOGICAL** argument is an a priori argument for the existence of God: scholars studied include **ANSELM** and **DESCARTES** with challenges put forward by **GAUNILLO** and **KANT**. Is it possible for God, once defined as lacking no imperfection, not to exist?

All the other arguments studied are **A POSTERIORI**; an argument based on, or after (post), empirical (observable) evidence. A posteriori arguments for the existence of God include:

The **COSMOLOGICAL** argument (argument from the existence of the cosmos) advocated by **AQUINAS** and **COPLESTON**, with challenges put forward by **HUME** and **RUSSELL**. Does the existence of the cosmos provide evidence for God as the Cause and as a **NECESSARY BEING**?

The **TELEOLOGICAL** argument (argument from the design and purpose of the world): **AQUINAS** and **PALEY** with challenges from **HUME**, **DARWIN** and **MILL**. Does the world have design and purpose and if so need a Designer?

In a category all by its own stands Kant's **MORAL ARGUMENT** (not an argument for the existence of God; **KANT** postulates or assumes the existence of God as a guarantor of the moral law), with challenges from **FREUD**. Does the existence of morality require a God who guarantees the **SUMMUM BONUM**?

CHALLENGES TO RELIGIOUS BELIEF

The **PROBLEM OF EVIL** and **SUFFERING**: What is meant by 'evil' and how is its existence compatible with a 'good' God? **THEODICIES** (the defence of the goodness of God in the face of evil and suffering) derive from **AUGUSTINE** and **IRANEAUS**, with challenges to these arguments.

RELIGION and **SCIENCE**: scientific understandings of the beginnings of the universe and explanations for design involve consideration of **DARWINISM, BIG BANG, CREATIONISM, INTELLIGENT DESIGN, IRREDUCIBLE COMPLEXITY**. Do scientific understandings about the cosmos challenge religious belief and, if so, how? Are religious responses to scientific theories which question faith convincing?

A NOTE ABOUT GOOD PHILOSOPHY OF RELIGION ESSAYS

See the Philosophy of Religion essay guide for more detailed help.

Good AS Philosophy of Religion essays will be ones that use arguments and avoid **ASSERTIONS** and assumptions. Philosophy is about clear and reasoned arguments; it is not about putting forward assertions, which really are just statements without any, let alone good, reasoning behind them. Here's an example of an assertion:

> 'Plato's Forms have no proof. If they existed we should be able to see them with our eyes, but where are they?'

I have seen this used in an essay, where someone is trying to say (notice, I haven't said argue, because this is not an argument) that the Realm of the Forms does not exist. It may not exist but this is not a strong way of going against Plato's argument, as it actually uses an **ASSERTION** rather than an **ARGUMENT**. The assumption behind this assertion is that 'everything that exists has to have physical 'proof.''* Imagine it was written like this:

- **PREMISE 1** - Everything that exists has physical proof for its existence

- **PREMISE 2** - Plato's Forms do not have physical proof

- **CONCLUSION** - Plato's Forms do not exist

Any decent philosophy student will spot that premise 1 is an **ASSUMPTION**, and the first question we should ask of such a premise is 'why?' There might be many things that exist that have no physical proof for them (there might not be, but you cannot just state that without saying why you are arguing for the physical proof worldview).

And, in fact, at this point really good philosophy students will be saying, 'the Realm of the Forms does not pretend to have physical proof for its existence, so why is this used against Plato's argument?'

Using assertions rather than arguments will cost you marks in this subject.

This is the Philosophy of Religion, not unreasoned opinions, assumptions, assertions or statements about religion.

Therefore, in all the sections that follow, try to see what the scholars are arguing and how they have supported those arguments with reasons. You are allowed your own view on the arguments you study, but you have to argue for or against the different scholars, not make simple assertions or unjustified statements that do not have reasoned foundations. Imagine moving from being a tabloid newspaper editor to being an editor of a broadsheet, and you will get the idea.

Essays will be better if you can argue with reasons, rather than make assumptions or assertions based on hunches or preferences.

A simple way of remembering these key points is the acronym **AREA**.

- **ARGUMENT/S** - Have I explained the argument (from Plato or Kant for example)? Have I shown the examiner that I comprehend what the scholar is saying and can clearly state the argument put forward?

- **RESPONSE/S** - Have I outlined and explained a good range of responses to the argument/s? Have I shown how these responses specifically challenge the original arguments? Have I shown how these counter-arguments work and how they relate to the question?

- **EVALUATION/S** - Now I have clearly set out positions, what do I think of these? This is not a case of saying what theory you like the most, as in a certain flavour of ice cream, but what you think is the better **PHILOSOPHICAL** argument and why. Does the original argument stand or fall against the criticisms raised here? Why or why not?

- **AND** ... This is something that is often missing in philosophy essays. Now I have analysed and evaluated arguments, what implications am I drawing? What is the 'and therefore' part of my essay? For example, you might be saying that you don't think a certain argument for the existence of God works, but if the theory was refined in a certain way or was able to address a particular criticism, it would come back stronger.

*'Proof' is not a word that some philosophers like to use – they are happy to say that they have argued for something, but they would not say that they have 'proved' that is the case.

Plato's Forms and Analogy of the Cave

KEY TERMS

- **METAPHYSICS** – the exploration of the fundamental nature of existence through questions such as, what is meant by 'reality'?

- **FORMS** (or ideals) – blueprints of things we see in this world. There is a Form for everything and every concept, such as truth. Forms are not physical 'mega' examples of a ball, or truth etc., but exist separately from the ball and truth, and are not just ideas we have thought of. Forms are 'real'; they are pure knowledge and are not dependent on opinions. Beauty is an idea in itself rather than what a person decides is a beautiful thing. But the beautiful thing would not exist if it did not participate in beauty in itself.

- **FORM OF THE GOOD** - at the top of a hierarchy of forms, this is the source of all knowledge; the form that gives each other form, like justice or chair, is its essential characteristic and nature.

- **ANALOGY** - where two things are compared as similar because they share common features (for example, the heart is like a pump).

- **UNIVERSALS** – the forms or ideals, such as the Universal form of a chair, or of justice; these do not exist in a physical sense, but are 'real' in the realm of the forms. They are unchangeable and exist beyond our perception of them.

- **PARTICULARS** – the objects we see, like this chair, that example of justice, which only have existence because they take part in the **UNIVERSAL** form of chair or justice. The individual particular object can change or be destroyed without affecting the Universal form of that thing. Particulars can be called **PHENOMENA** and Universals, **CONCEPTS**.

PLATO'S TWO WORLDS IN THE ANALOGY OF THE CAVE

Plato outlines his argument for two separate worlds in **THE REPUBLIC** and in several other works. He uses the **ANALOGY OF THE CAVE** to suggest that this world is one of shadows and darkness, of **APPEARANCES** and things that we can see and touch, hear, smell and feel, but this is not the 'real' world. The **REAL** world is where the **IDEALS**, or the **FORMS** of things, exist. We see many examples of things like chairs in this world (the cave world), but we only know that they are chairs because they bear some resemblance to the **FORM** of a chair, the **IDEAL** of a chair that exists in the **REALM OF THE FORMS**. The differences between the two worlds, the world of appearance and shadow, and the world of the forms, are outlined in the table below.

Plato's two worlds

(as demonstrated in the Analogy of the Cave)

THE WORLD OF SHADOWS	THE WORLD OF THE FORMS
Physical/material/exists in time and space	Spiritual
Illusion/world of appearance	Reality
Opinions, guesses and beliefs	**Knowledge**
Perceived by the senses	Known by reason/rational thought
Changeable (eg able to age and decay as things are physical)	Unchanging/consistent/eternal
Imperfect (seen as shadows)	Perfect (seen in the true light of knowledge)
Particular objects/'things'	Universal Forms/Ideals
Contingent/transient	Necessary/essential/permanent
Dependent on the sun (as represented by the fire)	Dependent on the Form of the Good

In some way the objects that we see in this world imitate their eternal Forms and therefore the objects bear some resemblance to the eternal Forms; they only have the reality they do have because of their participation in the Forms. It can be argued that Plato never really makes clear what he means by this participation.

In the **CAVE ANALOGY**, and in other writings, Plato is arguing that we often get confused and think that this world is the world of reality. Our **SOUL** is trapped in this body and forgets what the real world is, and because the things in this world are very immediate and appeal to our senses, we think that this is it, and are surprised by anyone who says there is more beyond the sensory world.

In the cave analogy, where people are chained up facing the back wall of a cave a long way under the ground, each part of the story symbolises something. Another chart below illustrates how.

THE EVENTS IN THE CAVE	WHAT THE EVENTS SYMBOLISE
Prisoners chained in a cave facing the back wall	People in this world trapped by physical appearances and sense experience. The cave itself represents this visible world. Plato thought that the body trapped the soul of a person. This world is illusory and does not offer knowledge.

People who are holding up statues or puppets behind the trapped prisoners; they hold these up in front of a fire and the fire casts shadows of these things on to the back wall.

The people who are seeing the shadows from the objects mistake them for real things. When they hear the voices of the people holding the objects rebounding off the walls, and see the shadows of the objects, it makes it feel to them like these are the sounds and sights of the real world and that is all there is. They are unaware of events taking place behind them as they are trapped looking at the back wall of the cave.

The people holding up the objects are also stuck in this world, and misleading people into accepting this world as the place of reality; possibly politicians and even supposed philosophers who do not pay attention to the realm of the forms.

The objects or statues that the people hold up represent images of the forms and are falsely being held up as real things.

A prisoner is freed and makes a difficult journey towards the entrance of the cave, getting used to different light, and stumbling his way towards the way out.

When a person realises that there is more to the world than what is immediately apparent. The philosophical journey of reason is not an easy one as it goes against the immediate sensations available to us and tends to cause us to 'see' the world in a different light.

The prisoner goes out of the cave and starts to see that a different world exists.

The prisoner realises the world he has been trapped in is illusory. Adjusting his eyes to the light he sees things like shadows of trees which are being cast by real objects (**FORMS**), behind which is the sun, which is the **FORM OF THE GOOD**. All of the forms are given existence by the form of the good. Reason informing the mind is essential for the philosopher to realise this, just as light on the eye is essential for him seeing things in this world.

The prisoner returns to the cave to tell the remaining prisoners that the cave is not the real world; they think he is out of his mind, as he is stumbling in the darkened cave after being in the light, and is killed.

The philosopher who tries to encourage a life of reason and suggests that this world is not reality will often face scorn and ridicule, and the death of the prisoner is a clear reference to the death of Plato's teacher, Socrates.

PLATO'S ARGUMENT FOR THE REALM OF THE FORMS

Plato argues for the world of the forms by asking us to think about our **PERCEPTION** of things: A red bus and a red shirt might look to be the same colour but are obviously different if looked at closely and in different lights. And yet we seem to be able to perceive a concept of 'redness' that links them and it could be argued that we have a consensus about what 'red' is. Plato argues that without this consensus and underlying stability of knowledge there would be no knowledge at all, if knowledge depended on us deciding what a thing was each time we looked at it.

Plato also puts forward an argument concerning our awareness of things such as perfection or mathematical truths which we have not been taught: no-one has ever seen a truly straight line, so we cannot say that we have gained such knowledge from empirical evidence. If this is the case, we must have some **KNOWLEDGE** of perfect straightness that has not been gained in this world.

In The Meno, **SOCRATES**, Plato's mentor, attempts to demonstrate that a slave boy with no training in mathematics can demonstrate mathematical knowledge, which must be due, he argues, from the distant memory of the forms stored within the **IMMORTAL SOUL**. This soul made the journey, rather traumatically, from the **REALM OF THE FORMS** across the 'river of forgetfulness', to be clothed in a body in this world and struggles to always recall what I would call '**FORM REALITY**', but the memory of such is still there.

Be aware that Plato's ideas do not just arise in a philosophical vacuum. He is very influenced by **PYTHAGORAS**' understanding that number is what constitutes ultimate reality, **PARMENIDES**' argument about a constant, unchanging universe and also **HERACLITUS**' metaphysical notions of change. Plato is attempting to bring ideas together in his metaphysics, where he questions and tries to understand ultimate reality.

STRENGTHS

- Plato might be correct in saying that we do search for 'ideas' and seem to have some vague idea that there are ultimate realities, which he calls the 'forms' of things.

- No one might have ever explained to us the connection between, for example, lots of different cats, but it could possibly be argued that we sense they belong together.

- Plato argues that our immortal soul 'knows' these forms as it existed in the realm of the forms before coming to the cave world. He argues that our soul has some 'knowledge' of what perfectly straight is even though we have never actually seen such in this world, and also the things we see in this world do bear at least some resemblance to the Forms/Ideals. And when we think about 'inventing' things, isn't it the case that we always have an idea first? Is Plato on to something when he says we have remembered that idea from the forms?

- Maybe our senses are as unreliable as Plato suggests. At least we can question if they are certain enough for us to build our world view upon them.

- Despite all the difficulties there are with Plato arguing for forms of the physical things we see around us, perhaps The Realm of Forms does work well with regard to concepts such as **JUSTICE**, **TRUTH** and **BEAUTY**. Does having ultimate forms of these overcome the difficulties of relativism and we stop asking what we think is good (for us) and instead find out what **ULTIMATE GOODNESS** is?

WEAKNESSES

- If Plato argues that things such as art and poetry are not conveyers of knowledge as they only imitate things in the world, then how strong is his own argument when it is based on an **ANALOGY**? And, because things work in an analogy, does that mean reality is like that analogy? For example, what link, precisely, is there between a form such as beauty and beautiful things? Does Plato need to spell that out more clearly?

- Is there a real danger that Plato so undermines this world that he actually devalues any experiences we have here and now; however, does our experience of daily life and things such as relationships, learning, making progress seem worthless? Is sense experience totally devoid of any worth?

- The **THIRD MAN** argument: Think about beds. Beds form a type of thing; because of this they have a Form – the Form of a Bed. But the Form of the Bed plus the beds form a new type of thing. They then need a new Form. Now that collection of things will need a Form and so on and so on.

KEY QUOTES

1. *'There is only one good, which is knowledge, and one evil, which is ignorance'. Plato*

2. *'No human thing is of serious importance'. Plato*

3. *'What is essential is invisible to the eye'. Saint-Exupéry*

4. *'Plato's 'ideas' are really just other particulars, ethically and aesthetically superior to the other kind'. Russell*

5. *'What on earth [do] the Forms contribute to sensible things [the objects we see and touch]? They cause neither movement or any change in them. To say that they are patterns and the other things share in them is to use empty words and poetical metaphors'. Aristotle*

6. *'A wise man proportions his belief to the evidence'. Hume*

7. *'It is not reason which is the guide of life, but custom'. Hume*

CONFUSIONS TO AVOID

- "Plato believed that the cave was a representation of what took place here and now, and the forms are like heaven" – this is not true. It is not helpful to use terms like heaven when writing about Plato. Although St. Paul in particular was heavily influenced by Plato, it is not correct to put things into Plato's mouth that he didn't say as otherwise you will make the examiner think you have not really understood that Plato was writing before Christianity and in response to Greek, not Christian, ideas.

- "Everything in an analogy has to work for an argument to work" – this is not true. The best analogies create helpful pictures for us to gain some understanding of an argument; however, they are never watertight, and, in fact, scholars do not always agree about what each element of the analogy of the cave means or is meant to refer to. This does not mean that we have to reject the entire argument, but we can ask if the analogy is successful in getting the general idea of the argument across. Examiners recognise that an analogy is what it is; they are more interested in if you think the argument it is representing works.

- When answering questions about Plato, students sometimes put down everything they know about the cave and the forms without answering the question. Questions are usually specific about either cave or forms, which does not mean you cannot bring in other elements of Plato's argument, but at all times the question must be the guide for why and how you bring things into your answers.

Aristotle

KEY TERMS

- **CAUSE** – Aristotle is interested in knowing what makes a thing the way it is and what causes things to move from potential to actual. Cause for Aristotle is not so much about what starts everything off, but how things change and what causes are involved in this process.

- **MATERIAL CAUSE** - the matter that things are made of – for example, a cricket bat has the material cause of a willow blade and a rubber grip on the handle.

- **EFFICIENT CAUSE** – the agent that causes the thing to come about, for example, the cricket bat maker who shapes the willow and therefore causes it to be a bat rather than part of a tree.

- **FORMAL CAUSE** – the actual thing that the object is being shaped into; the arrangement of the pieces of the object that make it the thing it is designed to be (its form or pattern). A rubber grip, tapered shoulders and a blade, which give it the characteristics, the Form, of a cricket bat.

- **FINAL CAUSE** – the function or purpose of the object's existence. The other causes work towards making something that will fulfil its purpose, which is the reason for which it is created; the cricket bat is made to score runs. This is its **TELOS** or end. Something is 'good' for Aristotle not when it takes part in the Form of Good, as Plato argued, but when it fulfils its function and reaches its telos.

- **MATTER AND FORM** – matter is what something is made out of. When it comes together, (through the **FOUR CAUSES** above) in a particular way, the object has certain characteristics, for example, the matter of a cricket bat is wood and rubber and these come together to form a run-scoring piece of sports equipment. The Form is the combined characteristics of that object (a run-scoring, ball-hitting bat) that make it clear what that object is. If it breaks, the matter stays the same but the form changes. Matter has potential to become different types of Forms depending on what the four causes work towards, so the willow from the tree could have become a bench rather than a cricket bat.

- **POTENTIAL TO ACTUAL** – when something undergoes a change from one state to another, eg, the cricket bat is an actual piece of willow, but it has the potential to become another actuality, a cricket bat, when it undergoes the causes outlined.

- **TELOS** – literally the end or goal; the end purpose or aim.

- **PRIME MOVER** – Aristotle's concept of God, the Unmoved Mover. It moves everything else from potential to actual; the Prime Mover causes all movement and change as things move towards it. It is perfect and not changing, and therefore is pure actuality.

ARISTOTLE'S FOUR CAUSES – AND ARISTOTLE ON PURPOSE

Aristotle differed from **PLATO** in arguing that it was possible to gain knowledge in and through the world of the senses. In studying **EMPIRICAL** evidence to try to understand the world, Aristotle was keen to find out how things existed and changed, and what things were made of – that is, what their essence consisted of. When he did this, he noticed, a posteriori, that all things can move from **POTENTIAL** to **ACTUAL**, and he was interested in finding out what **CAUSED** such change or movement.

In this process, Aristotle argued that **MATTER** can take on a new **FORM** (see above about the willow wood becoming a cricket bat), and have the characteristics of that **FORM**. Unlike Plato, Aristotle did not think these **FORMS** existed in a separate realm.

Within his work **METAPHYSICS**, Aristotle argued that there are four different but related causes that make something go from potential to actual.

All four causes are inextricably linked. The first cause of something is its **MATERIAL** or matter – what something is made out of. Aristotle looked at everyday objects (a block of marble was one particular object he wrote about), and noted that matter or material has the **POTENTIAL** to become something **ACTUAL**, to take on the **FORM** of something different. So, in asking the question what causes something to 'be' (which is a very prominent question in early Philosophy), Aristotle's first answer was the **MATERIAL** of which it was made.

However, this matter was then shaped by an **AGENT**, which could be a human being such as a sculptor or chef, or a natural agent such as the sea causing erosion. Aristotle called this the **EFFICIENT CAUSE**, and therefore he formed a more complete answer to his question about how things came to be, and how things changed from potentially being something to actually being something.

Material (marble) and efficient (sculptor) causes help to make something take shape, but there is also a pattern that the craftsman is working towards. They have a plan in mind which will mean that they get the rocking chair to actually take form from the matter with which they are working. Aristotle called this the **FORMAL CAUSE**.

The observer knows, when the item has reached its completion, that it is a rocking chair and not a table that the carpenter has made because it has the characteristics of the rocking chair – it has that **FORM** (within the individual object, rather than in a separate realm as part of a universal form of rocking chair, as Plato argued). And so, Aristotle saw more than one cause in how things moved from potential to actual – the material, how it was shaped and what form that caused it to be shaped in a particular way.

Aristotle argued that the material, efficient and formal causes are working towards creating an object that has a purpose.

The materials chosen, the way they have been put together, and the plan that helped the project reach its conclusion was all geared, Aristotle argued, to the **AIM** of the object reaching its **TELOS** or fulfilling its function. We can relate to this as we look at a new computer and ask, 'is it good?' When we are asking this, we are trying to find out how well it fulfils its purpose, and this was how Aristotle understood the word **GOOD** (which, again, is different to Plato).

Aristotle called this fulfilling of something's function the **FINAL CAUSE**.

So, in answering his question about what causes something to be, Aristotle argued that something comes fully to be when material, shape and form enabled it to fulfil its telos or goal. Aristotle argued that all things, including human beings, have **PURPOSE** - a final cause. Think for a moment of objects you can see around you right now, and identify the final cause of such objects; ask yourself if Aristotle is right to argue for this (incidentally, not knowing what the function or end aim of a thing is, is not the same as saying that it does not have a final cause).

To recap:

Once the material is shaped by an **EFFICIENT** cause or causes towards the plan or form, and the **FUNCTION** of an object (or human being) is realised, then potential has become actual, and the purpose of that object has been realised. This is not to say that the matter in that object might then be broken down and made into something else, but that would then fulfil a different function and again move from actual to potential in a new form.

ARISTOTLE'S PRIME MOVER

The **PRIME MOVER** should be seen as part of the argument from the four causes, just as the theory of the Forms is the backdrop to the analogy of the cave in Plato's work. Aristotle commences his **METAPHYSICS** from empirical evidence, through which he observes the four causes, and moves from there to the Prime Mover.

Because Aristotle has noticed that there is ongoing, continual change/motion in the universe, and individual things are moving from potential to actual, he now wants to understand both what makes things change in the first place, or instigates that change, and how the entirety of the universe is changing and **FULFILLING ITS PURPOSE**.

Aristotle wants to know if, ultimately, there is an efficient cause or something towards which everything is moving, which is not moved and who does not need to change.

This necessary something, which Aristotle calls an **UNMOVED MOVER** cannot be just the same as any other thing moving towards it telos as that would create a further problem of what caused that. This something is, for Aristotle, the **PRIME MOVER**.

Although it is correct to say that this is what Aristotle means by an eternal 'God' who is not reliant on anything else for existence, it is very clear that this is not a personal God, in the way in which God is understood in **GREEK** or **JUDEAO-CHRISTIAN** traditions, where God can be addressed using a personal pronoun such as he.

Aristotle's God is pure intelligence, non-physical (and therefore non-changing/decaying) fully realised actuality; it is unconcerned with the world (the prime mover would have to be unconcerned, as concern would change it, and it does not need to change – there is nothing for it to grow into, learn, improve or move towards).

It is true to say that the Prime Mover can do nothing but think of itself as it does not have any thought of something which does not have full actuality, which is anything else apart from itself.

The way in which THE **PRIME MOVER** is the mover of everything else is not so much in being the pusher of the first cause which then sets a chain reaction going off. **THE PRIME MOVER** is the thing towards which everything moves by attraction or desire – the movement from potentiality to what is ultimate actuality; in this sense it is a cause of movement, just as the cat moves towards the milk bowl without the milk bowl pushing the cat from behind.

THE PRIME MOVER is perfectly good in that it has full **ACTUALITY**, which means it lacks nothing, cannot change and is wholly simple. This influential idea is very different to the God of the Judaeo-Christian tradition.

STRENGTHS

- The idea of a **MATERIAL, EFFICIENT** and **FORMAL CAUSE** for objects is very accessible to many observers, particularly in a scientific age, where 'what things are made of', and 'how things come to be' are still relevant questions. Commencing with the **EMPIRICAL**, and suggesting that an object's Form is something that belongs to this realm, might seem like Aristotle has answered some objections to the problems in Plato's argument about a separate, **NON-PHYSICAL** realm of Forms, which is not accessible to our senses.

- When we look at everyday objects, can we can agree with Aristotle that there is a plan to which they have been made, in order for them to fulfil a **PURPOSE**? The chair you are sitting on right now is fulfilling the purpose for which it was made, with the appropriate materials chosen to complete the plan and take the **FORM** of a chair (there are problems with this view – see 1 and 2 below).

- Does the idea that things are in motion/changing seem something that can be supported? As we uncover more scientific knowledge, has Aristotle understood the world correctly in that things are always in the process of moving from **POTENTIAL** to **ACTUAL** and taking on the characteristics of new **FORM**?

WEAKNESSES

- Can it really be argued that the universe has a '**TELOS**'? It might be difficult to see how a universe has an end goal in mind. **RUSSELL** argued that the universe simply exists and does not have any overriding purpose. Even if things within the universe might apparently have a purpose, can we go from there to the whole and suggest the universe itself has a purpose?

- If we move 'within' the universe, then, again, it could be difficult to argue that things have a **TELOS. DAWKINS** argues that, through the process of natural selection, the fast predator catches the sick and deformed prey, and this helps both predator and prey, as the weak genes of the prey are filtered out, but the predator is ensured of a healthy future stock on which to feed.

- Dawkins argues there is no purposeful design behind evolution, or reasoning on the part of the animals.

- The problem gets worse when it is suggested that **INANIMATE** objects such as chairs have a 'purpose'; does it seems more likely that this purpose has been given to it by the maker of the chair rather than the chair having 'its own' purpose?

- Many have argued that the **PRIME MOVER** is irrelevant because it has no interaction with the universe, is not affected by it and is so unlike the universe or human beings that there is no shared experience between human beings and the thing which they ultimately desire. It is difficult to imagine an infinite series of causes, which is what Aristotle rejects by suggesting a Prime Mover; but difficulties in conceiving an idea is not a valid philosophical reason for rejecting it.

KEY QUOTES

1. *'There is a substance which is eternal and unmovable and separate from sensible things…..this substance is without parts and indivisible…impassive and unalterable'. Aristotle*

2. *'It [The Prime Mover] must be of itself that the divine thought thinks (since it is the most excellent of things) and its thinking is a thinking on thinking'. Aristotle*

3. *'God exists eternally, as pure thought, happiness, complete self-fulfilment, without any unrealised purposes. The sensible world, on the contrary, is imperfect, but it has life, desire, thought of an imperfect kind, and aspiration. All living things….are moved to action by admiration and love of God. Thus God is the final cause of all activity'. Russell outlining Aristotle's Prime Mover*

4. *'Even if it were true that each part of the human body serves a purpose, does it follow that the person as a whole has a purpose? Aristotle may be guilty of the error of composition, which is the mistake of assuming that because something is true of all the parts, the same must be true of the whole'. Wilkinson and Campbell*

5. *'You could give Aristotle a tutorial and you could thrill him to the core of his being. Aristotle was an encyclopaedic*

polymath, an all-time intellect, yet not only can you know more than him about the world, you can have a deeper understanding of how everything works. Such is the privilege of living after Newton, Darwin, Einstein, Planck, Watson, Crick and their colleagues'. Dawkins

6. *Aristotle's view that there is a purpose behind everything in nature, 'is not the nature of scientific reasoning today. We say that food and water are necessary conditions of life for man and beast. Had we not these conditions we would not have existed. But it is not the purpose of water or oranges to be food for us'. Gaarder*

CONFUSIONS TO AVOID

- "Aristotle argues that God is the First Cause" – his argument is more developed than that, and reference needs to be given to his desire to explain motion/cause and purpose. Links between the four causes and the Prime Mover are necessary and must be explained rather than simply outlined.

- "Aristotle rejects the idea of forms" – not true. He does not think that forms exist separate from the object, which is a major departure from Plato.

Judeao-Christian Influences upon the Philosophy of Religion

KEY TERMS

- **CREATOR** – one who makes, as in God creating the universe.

- **CREATIO EX NIHILO** – creation from nothing, or out of nothing.

- **CRAFTSMAN** – one with the skills to design or mould or craft materials into something.

- **OMNIPOTENT** – literally 'all power', but has been interpreted by many scholars, when referenced to God, as a being who can do 'all things logically possible'.

- **OMNISCIENT** – literally 'all knowledge'; knowledge of all things past, present and future.

- **OMNIPRESENT** – literally 'all present'. God - a being who is in all places at all times.

- **TRANSCENDENT** – above and beyond, outside and independent from the material universe, with reference to God.

- **IMMANENT** – God intimately present in the universe.

- **DEISM** – the belief that God created the universe but is no longer involved in sustaining or intervening in it.

- **THEISM** – the belief that God created and continues to be involved in the sustenance of the universe, and intervenes in it.

- **EUTHYPHRO's DILEMMA** – the problem posed by the question of whether God commands things because they are good, or whether they are good because He commands them. Divine Command Theory is the name given to the second position.

The Philosophy of Religion in the West has been influenced by ideas and beliefs within the **JUDEAO-CHRISTIAN** tradition. The following covers the concepts of God as creator and the goodness of God and how these ideas are similar to, differ from, and are influenced by, GREEK ideas.

GOD AS CREATOR

The way The Bible presents God as involved with his creation

Many scholars point out the limitations of language when talking and writing about God, an 'other-worldly Being'. This is covered more at A2, but it can be useful to note such challenges involved in expressing concepts adequately.

Many scholars and believers within the **JUDEAO-CHRISTIAN** tradition do not reject **SCIENTIFIC** accounts of the formation of the universe, and argue that such accounts are **COMPATIBLE** with teachings found in the **BIBLE** and their traditions. However, within this tradition it is argued that scientific accounts do not tell the whole story as the creation is the loving act of a creator who is intimately involved in both the creation and sustaining of the universe.

Immediately, this sets up a contrast with Aristotle's **PRIME MOVER**, who has nothing to do with the created world, having no relationship with something that has not reached its actuality. Rather than address the differences as a separate topic, this revision guide draws attention to the contrasts between the Prime Mover and the Judeao-Christian understandings of God throughout the next section.

Whilst no specific Biblical texts are given for study, candidates are expected to give examples of the concepts they are describing. The creation accounts in Genesis 1-3 demonstrate the concept of an **INVOLVED CREATOR**. Within Genesis God is seen to be 'hovering over the waters', moving and shaping material – *indicating* a God who acts to instigate and design creation (it has His hallmark, like a jeweller stamps their designs).

God commands things to come into being, like light and stars, plants, animals and human beings ('God said' something and it happened; think how a parent tells a child to tidy their bedroom and it happens) – *indicating* both the relationship and involvement God has with his creation.

God forms **ADAM** (meaning earth person) and **EVE** (meaning mother of living things or life), in his image, so that something of the character of God is seen in his finest creation, humanity – *indicating* God's desire that his nature is shown in the universe. He appoints Adam and Eve, representing humanity, as **STEWARDS** (caretakers on behalf of God) of creation – *indicating* God's ongoing care for and interest in the development of creation.

God is concerned when Adam and Eve disobey instructions for their well-being; God is described as 'walking in the garden' – *indicating* a close involvement or **IMMANENCE** which is expressed in personal/relational terms.

Other texts indicate that God **GIVES ORDER** within creation; **PSALM 8** says God has placed man over the 'works of his hands' - *indicating* purposeful involvement and giving of structure by the creator. **PSALM 147** says that God determines the number of stars – *indicating* intimate knowledge of the creation by the creator. **ISAIAH 40** notes God's ongoing control over all of creation – *indicating* interested governorship (school governors are more influential on a school than most students realise; decisions they make are, hopefully, out of concern for the school's welfare and ongoing success and such decisions require governors to be involved with the school). Again, see the contrast between this idea and the **PRIME MOVER**.

In the story of the Israelites, God's giving of a **COVENANT** shows concern for the development of humanity; this will be covered under the section concerning God's goodness.

Many of the Biblical texts above support:

The imagery of God as craftsman

GENESIS 1 and **2** give different accounts of the creation of the universe and how God literally crafts and shapes something which was viewed as being '**FORMLESS AND VOID**.' It is well worth reading those chapters for this section.

In **ISAIAH 40** God measures the water; in **PSALM 139** God crafts the human being in the mother's womb; **JOB 38** (pronounced jobe) gives a long list of God's work, including the shaping of the earth like clay, the setting of the constellation pleiades and the ordering of the day; **JEREMIAH 18** describes God as a potter, **PSALM 127** as a builder, both crafts requiring specific skills of planning and attention to detail.

Whilst this picture of **CRAFTSMAN** certainly would indicate some purpose in the created order, as Aristotle suggests, and both the Judeo-Christian and Aristotelian ideas state that the universe would not be here were it not for God, the **PERSONAL** nature in which the Bible records God creating and crafting the universe is very different to how the **PRIME MOVER** is portrayed, which is like some impersonal cosmic magnet to which all motion is inevitably attracted. God as crafstman also seems aware, knowledgeable about and interested in the world in a way the prime mover is not. But, in contrast to God's immanent nature (his close involvement in the world), God as craftsman is also seen as above and separate from the universe; this demonstrates his **TRANSCENDENT** nature, which arguably is similar to **ARISTOTLE**'s view.

The Judeo-christian tradition regards God as both immanent and transcendent at the same time.

The final comment above starts to look more closely at the **ATTRIBUTES OF GOD** in the Judeao-Christian tradition, where God is understood to be **OMNIPOTENT**, **OMNISCIENT** and **OMNIPRESENT**.

The **OMNIPOTENCE** of God has been understood differently by different scholars, and Greek ideas of power have influenced these ideas. **DESCARTES** argued that God's **OMNISCIENCE** means God can do anything at all, even that which is not logically possible. If he could not do that, he would not be all-powerful.

AQUINAS and **LEWIS** both argued that the term means that God can do everything that is **LOGICALLY POSSIBLE**, as to do that which is not logically possible (like make a ball completely red and completely blue at the same time, or make 3+3=4) is asking God to do a nothing, literally a no thing, and that is never a possibility as it is 'not a something'. No power at all could do such a thing as it could never exist in any world.

Whilst the Bible talks of God being 'powerful' and states, in 2 **CHRONICLES 20** that 'power and might are in God's hand', meaning that 'no one can withstand God', it hints at, rather than directly states, that God is omnipotent. This term shows the influence of **GREEK IDEAS** and regular demonstrations of the power of the Gods over the development of Judeo-Christian tradition (note that different nations sometimes had to show that 'our God is more powerful than your God' in order for them to survive).

However, some scholars have argued that it takes an all-powerful being to create the universe and also do things such as make the sun stand still as in **JOSHUA 10**. Importantly, the Judaeo-Christian tradition believes that God's power operates within the framework of **LOVE** and **GOODNESS**, so it is not like a dictatorship.

The **OMNISCIENCE** of God, in a traditional sense, means that there is nothing that has happened, is happening, or will happen that God does not know of. This idea has enormous implications, which are more developed at A2. In **ACTS 2**, it states that Jesus was given over to the authorities, 'by God's **FOREKNOWLEDGE**.' Many of the texts used in the creation section, such as **JOB 38,** speak about God knowing everything there is to know about creation, and humanity. In **PSALM 139**, the author writes, 'before a word is on my tongue you know it completely.' In the last judgement in **REVELATION 22**, God knows every act ever done.

The **OMNIPRESENCE** of God simply means that God is present everywhere at all times; again this seemingly straightforward idea is developed more at A2. The idea is most clearly stated in **PSALM 139**, where the author writes, 'where can I go from your presence?' before listing places far and wide, and various heights and depths, where he cannot escape God's presence. Again, the idea of 'God in' his creation in a personal kind of sense, or the **IMMANENCE** of God, stands in contrast to Aristotle's **PRIME MOVER**.

If God is omnipotent, omniscient and omnipresent, as well as being a craftsman did he create the universe **EX NIHILO**, that is, out of nothing?

This idea has a long history which developed over time but is a concept alien to Greek philosophy; as such it deserves further study than possible here. **CREATIO EX NIHILO** is not an idea that is straightforwardly apparent in Genesis 1 and 2, where **EXISTING MATERIAL** ('the earth was formless') is given its shape by God. It could be argued that God brings order from chaos in such stories rather than creates from scratch, and **CREATIO EX NIHILO** as a belief is developed in later Christian thought, rather than in the Jewish tradition. (Note that there is no philosophical argument for the existence of God in the Bible. He is assumed to pre-exist everything else). **CREATION EX NIHILO** is important in two ways: does it tie in with the scientific understanding of time and space beginning at the Big Bang? And, what implications does it have for the presence of evil in the world if God makes everything from nothing?

As creator is God responsible for everything in the Universe?

If God is **CREATOR** and **CRAFTSMAN**, as well as **OMNIPOTENT** and **OMNISCIENT**, it might be argued that he is **RESPONSIBLE** for everything that takes place in the universe, just as the creator and designer of a product might be seen to be ultimately responsible for the success or failure of that item. Issues and questions that arise here:

1. God is both to blame for apparently bad design in the world, such as earthquakes and to thank for apparently good design in the world, such as a beautiful lake.

2. God is responsible for the presence of both good and evil.

3. In what sense does humanity bear any responsibility for their actions if God knows what they are going to do? To what extent is humanity responsible for good and evil?

4. Are there differences between what we understand to be a **CRAFTSMAN** of something such as a table, using existing materials and design ideas, and the idea of creation and crafting from nothing?

5. What are the different ways of understanding **OMNIPOTENCE** and **OMNISCIENCE**, and what bearing would those different understandings have in this area?

6. Some **DEISTS*** argue that the existence of the universe itself is what God is responsible for, not the actions of those within it, or what the actions of nature (such as volcanic eruptions) result in.

7. Dawkins argues that attributing to God the responsibility for the universe is from a time when humanity did not understand the **NATURAL ORDER** or laws of science, and now science has developed such knowledge, we should take responsibility for a God-less universe.

The above issues offer interesting points of contrast when considering Aristotle's **PRIME MOVER** and **JUDEO-CHRISTIAN** understandings of God. In the former, a ****DEIST** view is held, where God is responsible for the initial creation of the universe, but has no ongoing relationship with or concern for it. Some scientists hold this view, and suggest that God is the first cause. In the **JUDEAO-CHRISTIAN** perspective, a **THEIST** view argues that God is not just the first cause, but continues to sustain the universe, and is interested in its well-being, even responding to prayer. Some scientists also hold this view. This is studied in more detail at A2.

The Goodness of God

The **GOODNESS** of God is a consistent theme in the **JUDEAO-CHRISTIAN** tradition. The Bible, and particularly the Psalms (see Psalms 145 and 100) declare that God is **ALL GOOD** and **ALL LOVING**, through both the act of creation and the goodness of nature, as well as his ongoing care, even though his actions are not always understood. The **JEWISH TRADITION** understands that throughout the history of Israel written in the **TORAH** God's actions in the world demonstrated his **GOODNESS** to them, including miraculous deliverance of them to safety in many difficult situations. In the Christian tradition, God's goodness is seen in giving his son Jesus to live as an example and then to die for humanity.

GOD AS MORALLY PERFECT AND A SOURCE OF HUMAN ETHICS

RICHARDS notes that two Hebrew words are used several times in the Old Testament to celebrate the goodness of God: **HESED**, meaning loving kindness or merciful compassion and **RAHAMIN**, meaning a gut-feeling response of tender pity that is evoked in a mother by her child. In addition, the Greek **AGAPE**, unconditional love, is used to express Christian understanding of the goodness of God. The correct understanding of the previous attributes discussed (the 'omnis') must be filtered through, or held in balance with, this idea of the goodness of God; a further addition must be considered in that the bible is keen to stress the justice of God. **PSALM 116** states that the Lord is just in all his ways and kind in all his doings.

Bearing the above in mind, with ultimate goodness, power, knowledge and justice combined, God's nature is understood as morally perfect, and hence he has authority to issue commands which are the source of human ethics. He does this in the context of a **COVENANT RELATIONSHIP** with Israel, where He outlines a two-way agreement between Himself and Israel for how they should live. It should be noted that because the Judeo-Christian tradition holds (mainly) a **THEIST** understanding of God, his ongoing desire for **CREATION** to flourish helps explain why God would enter into a **COVENANT** and give ethical commands for how humanity should live.

The above preamble sets the scene for God to issue **COMMANDS**, as seen in the 613 (not just 10) outlined in **EXODUS**, that would govern every aspect of Jewish life.

Commands were given to demonstrate and exemplify the perfect moral goodness and justice of an involved creator, and to help Israel become established as a morally good and just nation.

The standard expected from a **MORALLY PERFECT** God is high, with clear instruction that those who follow a good God should treat others, particularly the poor and marginalised, with compassion and ethical integrity; clear notice is also given to the results of either following or disregarding these commandments, which indicates how serious they are seen to be. **CHRISTIANS** (it is vital here that a student does not refer to the Judeo-Christian tradition at this point, but separates the two religions) believe that the morally perfect example was seen in the **INCARNATION** of Christ, who embodied God's nature, and therefore the goodness and justice of God. Christians would therefore view the teaching and life of Christ as demonstration of how the teaching of the Old Testament should be lived out in a life of **MORAL INTEGRITY**. Christ's teaching becomes a key source of ethics for Christians.

GOD AS BOTH LAWGIVER AND JUDGE

Some of the imagery of the Bible that perhaps best outlines these ideas is that of God as a **PARENT**, who lays down a good set of laws, in a loving and concerned manner, laws which are supposed to develop the child and help them understand appropriate boundaries. At the same time the parent acts as a **JUDGE** and 'consequence-giver' when the law is broken, as without consequences the law is seen as worthless and the consistency and character of the **LAW-GIVER** called into question. In this way, God's goodness is seen in the fair setting (**LAWGIVING**) and application (**JUDGING**) of the law. In the Christian tradition, Jesus is seen as one who suffers the punishment of the breaking of the law by humanity. **GOD**, the **JUDGE**, allows His son die to demonstrate his goodness in dying on behalf of humanity.

In consideration of the idea of God as law-giver in the Bible, the question is raised:

Does God command things because they are good or are things good because God commands them?

This question is found in Plato's dialogue **EUTHYPHRO** (hence **EUTHYPHRO'S** DILEMMA) where Socrates asks Euthyphro, "is the pious loved by the Gods because it is pious, or is it pious because it is loved by the Gods?"

In Philosophy, this is known as a dilemma, or when we are placed on the 'horns of a dilemma', as the two different options each provide difficulties, and we are faced with a sharp 'horn' on both sides. If it is decided that God commands things because they are good, then a standard of goodness exists outside of, and above, God's decision about what is good and bad. God simply agrees with what is already good and therefore this challenges the notion that he is the one who classifies what is morally good. God no longer seems **OMNIPOTENT** in this case.

If this leaves the second option, which is known as **THE DIVINE COMMAND THEORY**, that things are good because God commands them, we also face a difficulty. If God alone classifies what is good, then his judgement could simply be that rape and murder is good – if God says that it is, then it must be, as there is no **INDEPENDENT** standard of goodness against which to judge such a decision (precisely because we have rejected that option on the other 'horn').

This makes goodness **ARBITRARY**, based simply on the whim of a God who doesn't negotiate.

Both options raise problems. In the first option, God is not the one who decides what moral goodness is, which challenges the idea of God being all-powerful and the source of ethics; in the second, God could command anything and it become good precisely because He has commanded it. How can this problem be solved?

Aquinas argued that both can be accepted because God knows what to command due to his omniscience and his commands will be good due to his **OMNIBENEVOLENCE** (all-goodness). In other words, if God is **INTRINSICALLY** good and the source of all goodness, His nature will only issue that which He perfectly knows to be good. Thus it could be that this is not a problem at all; as **RICHARDS** notes, goodness is precisely what God is identified with, and the idea of God existing without goodness and vice versa is absurd.

STRENGTHS: God as Creator

- Certain interpretations of the creation accounts might result in some **SHARED GROUND** between religion and science.

- The Judeo-Christian tradition argues that the concept of an uncreated source as creator, has **LOGICAL APPEAL** and is needed to bring existence into being.

- The concept of an **INVOLVED CREATOR**, crafting and working and interested in the progress of creation and humanity, is a wide-spread and hard-wearing belief. This does not make it right, but it has appealed in a more consistent way than Aristotle's Prime Mover, which can be regarded as too distant a concept to be called 'God' as that word is understood across major world religions.

WEAKNESSES

- Is it possible to say God is a skilled craftsman based on the evidence from a world which includes **NATURAL EVILS** such as regular drought, flooding and illnesses caused by natural causes?

- Do humans have **FREE WILL** if God is all-knowing, and if God gives a set of commandments for how to live?

- Does the evidence of the world suggest God is **OMNIPOTENT** and omniscient?

STRENGTHS: Goodness of God

- It could be argued that an external source of ethics helps solve the difficulties raised by relative morality.

- Has Aquinas successfully solved **EUTHYPHRO'S DILEMMA**, by arguing God is both omniscient and omnibenevolent?

- Where do we get our sense of goodness from? Can accounts of a source of goodness give more successful answers to this than science, which might not be fitted for answering such a question?

WEAKNESSES

- Some of the actions of God in the Bible, such as the destruction of entire cities, including women and children in **JOSHUA 1-8**, do not seem 'good' but arbitrary and unfair, which would challenge the notion of God as fitting the profile of the source of morality and a good judge.

- Does the nature of the world suggest God is good, or is there too much **SUFFERING** to support such a claim? Is the history of the Jewish people enough to suggest God is good, considering the many persecutions they have faced?

- Is Aquinas' 'solution' to **EUTHYPHRO**'s dilemma adequate? Does it act as a statement of faith to which the evidence is made to fit? God knows what is good because he is all-knowing, and because he is all-knowing knows what is good, seems like a circular statement.

KEY QUOTES

1. *'In the beginning God created the heavens and the earth, and the earth was without form and empty'. Genesis 1*

2. *'From everlasting to everlasting is the Lord's love with those who keep his covenant and remember to obey his laws'. Psalm 103*

3. *'Sparrows are sold two for a penny, but not one of them falls to the ground outside your Father's care'. Jesus*

4. *'God will judge between nations and settle disputes for strong nations far and wide'. Micah 4*

5. *'Creator of all things invisible and visible....who from the very beginning of time and by his omnipotent power made from nothing creatures both spiritual and corporeal'. Fourth Lateran Council*

6. *'Both scriptural routes....encourage a system of morals which any civilised modern person, whether religious or not, would find – I can put it no more gently – obnoxious'.*

7. *'I cannot conceive of a God who rewards and punishes his creatures'. Einstein*

8. *'Maybe there isn't a God after all; maybe there's only a*

universe rotating by itself like a millstone'. Gao Xingjan

9. *'Theologians and philosophers, who make God the creator of Nature and the architect of the Universe, reveal Him to us as an illogical and unbalanced Being. They declare He is benevolent because they are afraid of Him, but they are forced to admit that His ways are vicious and beyond understanding'. France*

CONFUSIONS TO AVOID

- When writing about the 10 commandments, note that these are not stand alone instructions, but only make sense in the context of God developing the nation of Israel through **COVENANT**. They are seen by Jews and Christians as something of the expression of the nature of a personal, immanent God who desires humanity's best. They are not the only example of law-giving in the bible, and for Christians (but not Jews) the goodness and justice of God is ultimately seen in the life, death and resurrection of Jesus, who exemplifies a morally perfect life.

- Do not merely **DESCRIBE** God's attributes, such as goodness, omnipotence, omniscience – the question will normally ask you to show that you understand how these terms are explained in the Bible and what implications there might be if God does have such attributes.

- Don't give the impression that terms such as omnipotence, craftsman, goodness, law-giver and concepts such as Aristotle's Prime Mover and Euthyphro's dilemma are simple and by putting them in your answer you have somehow shown that you know what they mean. Reading around these terms will enable you to see how they work together or conflict and what they mean in context, which will help you develop an answer that provides **ANALYSIS** rather than a shopping list of terms.

- Be very clear on the distinct **DIFFERENCES** between Greek philosophical ideas of God and Judeo-Christian beliefs. There are differences involving the understanding of God as immanent and transcendent, personal and impersonal, what 'good' means in different arguments from Plato, Aristotle and the Judeo-Christian tradition; the creation stories are accepted, by faith, as revelatory of God's character within the Judeo-Christian tradition, which is again different to Greek understandings.

Traditional Arguments for the Existence of God

KEY TERMS

- **ONTOLOGICAL** – words or wisdom (logos) about being (ontos). What it means for something to be.

- **A PRIORI** – knowledge gained prior to experience.

- **A POSTERIORI** – knowledge gained after experience.

- **DEDUCTION** - a type of reasoning whereby it is demonstrated that the conclusion necessarily follows from the premises (as seen in the Ontological argument).

- **INDUCTION** – a type of reasoning that takes specific instances and from them, draws a general conclusion (eg. as seen in the Cosmological argument).

- **NECESSARY BEING** – a being whose non-existence is a contradiction.

- **CONTINGENT EXISTENCE** – something which, by its nature, does not necessarily have to exist, and could or could not have existence, eg you or me. Once existent, can go out of existence.

- **PREDICATE** – a property of a subject, for example. tall, round; for Anselm, necessary existence is a predicate of the greatest possible being.

- **ANALYTIC STATEMENT** – a statement where the predicate is contained within the subject, eg married men are husbands, or, for Anselm, God (subject) necessarily exists (predicate).

- **SYNTHETIC STATEMENT** – a statement where the predicate is not contained with the subject, eg married men are happy, and some knowledge of the world is required to assess its validity.

- **REDUCTIO AD ABSURDUM** – an argument that shows that the opposite of what it is claiming cannot be true.

- **IMMUTABLE** – not capable or susceptible to change; unalterable

The Ontological argument (OA) for the existence of God (a title **KANT** gave to this argument) is the only argument studied that does not start from empirical evidence and work back to God (the latter types of arguments are **A POSTERIORI** and inductive in nature). The OA commences with a definition of God given by **ANSELM** which, once understood, entails actual (and then in a later argument) **NECESSARY** existence.

ANSELM's ONTOLOGICAL ARGUMENT

The first form of the argument is found in Prosologion (Discourse on the Existence of God) chapter 2:

- God is the greatest possible being that can be thought of.

- If God exists only in the mind (or understanding) then a greater being could be conceived to exist both in the mind and in reality.

- This 'greatest possible being' (of premise one) must therefore exist in the mind and in reality.

Therefore God must exist as a being in reality (in re) as well as in the mind (in intellectu).

Anselm was writing with reference to **PSALMS 14** and **53** where it notes that 'the fool says in his heart there is no God.' He stated that the fool understood that God is 'that than which nothing greater can be conceived.'

Anselm argued that the fool, once he understood this, logically had to acknowledge that it was not possible for such a being to exist in thought alone as then there would be a greater being who existed in thought and reality.

Anselm noted that it would be **CONTRADICTORY** to state, once the fool has in his mind the greatest possible being, that such a being cannot exist, as existence in reality is an intrinsic quality in the greatest being (by definition). Therefore God exists.

Chapter 3 of the Prosologion developed this argument by stating again that God is the greatest possible being, and that, as such, has

NECESSARY EXISTENCE. God cannot not be, and a necessary state of being is always greater than **CONTINGENT EXISTENCE**, which is dependent on other things for existence (again, think you or me). If the state of necessary existence is greater than contingent existence, and God is the greatest possible being, God must be, uniquely, a **NECESSARY** being, entirely not dependant on anything else for existence, ie intrinsically necessary.

Something having the possibility of not existing or coming in and going out of existence – a **CONTINGENT** being – will always be less than that which cannot not exist. Anselm's claim was that the predicate of existence is an intrinsic part of the concept of God just as a spinster has the predicate of 'being unmarried' (this will be important later when **KANT** critiques Anselm), and this type of argument, where the **PREDICATE** (exists necessarily) is contained in the **SUBJECT** (God) is known as an **ANALYTIC STATEMENT**. The idea of God not existing is a logical impossibility and hence Anselm's argument is a **REDUCTIO AD ABSURDUM**. Remember that this is an argument based on the consideration of the very 'beingness' or intrinsic nature of God, not on a posteriori evidence from the world that may lead us to conclude there is a God.

GAUNILO'S CHALLENGE TO ANSELM'S ARGUMENT AND ANSELM'S REPLY

GAUNILO, a French monk and contemporary to Anselm, wrote On Behalf of the Fool as a response to Anselm. He argued that someone could imagine something like a beautiful island, and think that this was the most excellent, **PERFECT** island. Using Anselm's reasoning, Gaunilo argued that for the island to really be the greatest island it must exist in reality as well as in the imagination. If it did not exist in reality it would not be the greatest island. You can apply Gaunilo's point here to anything and say because it is perfect it must exist in reality not just in the mind.

Gaunilo said that this island obviously does not exist just because we have imagined it to be so, defined it as the greatest and then said that because it is the greatest that means it must have existence. Gaunilo suggested that those who believe such an island existed because of this reasoning are either joking or foolish, and anyone who believed them would likewise be a **FOOL**. He used this counter-example to challenge Anselm on his argument for God's existence which, as outlined above, goes along similar lines, and, Gaunilo suggests, is as flawed as the argument for the island's existence.

We cannot just define things into existence.

ANSELM'S REPLY TO GAUNILO

Gaunilo's criticism concentrates on the first formulation of **ANSELM**'s argument about things existing in the mind and reality. In Anselm's Reply to Gaunillo he emphasised that the island he used in his example is **CONTINGENT**, and would never have to exist in the way that God as a necessary being has to, as the greatest thing that can be thought. It is logically conceivable to think that the island could not exist, unlike God.

God as the greatest thing that can be thought is, by his very nature, in a category of one, and is something that cannot not exist or be greater or bettered.

The island however could always have one more palm tree, or a bluer sea, and could either not exist, or exist without perfection as that is not something of its intrinsic nature. **PLANTINGA** noted that, unlike the greatest being that can be thought of, God, islands have no **INTRINSIC** maximum. A contingent island and a necessary God cannot be compared.

DESCARTES' ONTOLOGICAL ARGUMENT

In Meditation 5 of Meditations on Philosophy, Descartes built on his previous thought that certain truths are, by their very nature, impossible to be doubted, and that people are innately able to understand that some things cannot be different, ie, equality and shape. He thought that one **INNATE IDEA** people had was a concept of God as a perfect being.

Working from this and drawing on his background as a mathematician, Descartes argued that there are certain things that have an unchangeable nature, and we know that this is the case. He used the example of a triangle. Essential to its nature are 'three angles equal to two right angles', and the nature of the triangle could not be different; it is **IMMUTABLE**.

God's nature is likewise immutable and part of that **IMMUTABLE NATURE** is having all perfections, of which one is existence. Triangles have essential characteristics, without which they would not be triangles; God has the essential characteristic of existence, without which such a being could not be God.

However, what if it could be argued that we can think of a triangle which has to have certain characteristics for it to be a triangle, but then acknowledge that such a triangle doesn't have to exist in reality? **DESCARTES** noted this but said that existence is a perfection, and as God, by definition and as part of his essence, has all perfections, he has to exist in a way that a triangle has to have internal angles of 180°.

It is a contradiction to claim otherwise, but it is simply that the triangle doesn't have existence as one of its necessary essences, whereas God does.

(Note here that Descartes is claiming that existence is 'more perfect' than non-existence, as Anselm said existence was part of the greatest being). An object has to have certain **NECESSARY** things for it to be that object; it cannot be separated from those characteristics. Descartes used a further example of a mountain which cannot exist without a valley; likewise, it is not possible to talk of God (and God alone, not any contingent items) without perfection, and existence is a **PERFECTION**.

KANT'S OBJECTIONS

Kant argued that existence is not a **PREDICATE** like green or tall. The latter help to describe the object. 'Existence' cannot be used in that way, as existence refers to the whole object.

All that Descartes has done is to say, if a triangle exists it has interior angles adding up to 180°; similarly Kant argued that the **ONTOLOGICAL ARGUMENT** says, if God exists he is a necessary being, but this does not mean he does exist in reality.

Kant's argued that 'existence is not a predicate.' A **PREDICATE** is something that adds to our knowledge of what a subject is like, for example, such a thing is big or brown or flat. **EXISTENCE** doesn't work in this way, as it does not tell us anything about the object that helps us in the identification of that object. Existence is actually the thing and all its characteristics, rather than just another predicate.

For example, if I say that my boat is fast, I give more information about the boat, but if I say the boat exists then I add nothing to the description of it; I am actually saying that there is a real example of this boat, and this is not what the role of a predicate is. Try this in reverse: If I say, 'the boat does not exist' then I have not actually just taken away one property (or predicate) of the boat but have taken away the entire boat.

What **KANT** noted was that when we say something exists we are saying that such an object has been **ACTUALISED**, but he argued that we cannot simply add existence to the concept of God and say we have proved or actualised the existence of such a concept. Noting the essential characteristics of a triangle as certain angles only actually gets us as far as saying, 'IF a triangle existed it would have these characteristics.'

Believing that God exists, and, following on from that belief to say that God has necessary existence, is not an argument that God necessarily has to exist in reality, just like triangles do not have to have existence, although if they did they would have certain predicates.

If there is a God, he has necessary existence, but the predicate of necessary existence cannot be declared as intrinsic to God and a claim made that as a consequence God has to exist in reality.

Kant thus argues that it is not contradictory to think of a possible being who has **NECESSARY** existence. To describe something as having characteristics would give us a picture of something if it existed, but by describing something, even by saying something has necessary existence, does not establish the existence of that thing. For Kant, all statements about existence are **SYNTHETIC**, true or false after verification, and not analytic, meaning 'true by nature'. The existence of God needs to be verified from a position exterior to the concept as it were, not by **ANALYTIC** analysis of the term.

If **ANSELM** and **DESCARTES** think they have overcome this idea by suggesting that God has necessary existence as one of the characteristics of the greatest or perfect being, and only this predicate can be assigned to God, then they are in danger of making a circular argument. Are they suggesting that God exists necessarily on the grounds that God has necessary existence?

Has Descartes convinced you that necessary existence has to entail actual existence? Or, as **CATERUS** argued, is this not enough and Descartes still has to show that the 'concept of necessary existence entails actual existence' (in Lacewing).

A modern day reply to Kant has come from **NORMAN MALCOLM**.

After outlining the idea of an unlimited being as one that does not depend on anything for its existence (meaning God is not contingent), and also that if God does not exist then he cannot come into existence, Malcolm put forward the following formulation:

- The existence of an unlimited being is either logically impossible or logically necessary.

- God's existence is not logically impossible, as there is no logical contradiction in the concept of a God/unlimited being who exists (the idea is not logically absurd or internally contradictory).

- God's existence is therefore logically necessary.

But again, has Malcolm answered the key problem of whether the concept of God as necessary entails existence in reality? Does it mean that if the existence of God is not impossible, it is **NECESSARY**, or just **POSSIBLE**? (It is worth reading the Malcolm extract at the end of the chapter).

Scholars have noted that Malcolm may have proved the concept of the **LOGICAL NECESSITY** of God's existence (that the non-existence of God is a logical impossibility and self-contradictory), but not the existence of God in reality or factually.

Words and concepts do not always describe realities, even when those concepts have internal and logical consistency.

STRENGTHS

- There is some attraction to a **DEDUCTIVE** and **ANALYTIC** argument that appeals to logical consistency rather than the mixed evidence for God from a posteriori evidence. It is an argument that has received much attention due to the fact that there does seem something to be wrong with it, but what that something is, is not always apparent.

- Anselm and Descartes both responded to criticism that was levelled at their versions of the OA, and stressed what it means for God to be the **GREATEST POSSIBLE BEING** and necessary by definition. Examples of the greatest or perfect contingent things might therefore not count against what Anselm and Descartes argued. Some have argued that with Malcolm's reformulation of the OA, the argument still holds importance.

- Does Kant's critique of Descartes' OA hold? It might be that saying that 'something exists', for example, Spiderman, does add something new to the description because up until that point the listener would have been thinking of a fictional character. Jackson points out that the atheist may be thinking of God as a fictional character so the addition of 'and exists' may actually change the definition of the word God, and thus existence, in that sense, may act as a predicate.

WEAKNESSES

- Prosologion is written by a monk as a prayer – can it be used as an argument for the existence of God? Rather, is it a support to those who already believe? Is it, more properly, **FAITH SEEKING UNDERSTANDING**?

- Is existence in reality **NECESSARILY** and in all cases greater than existence in the mind only? This is a value judgement. Are there counter examples to this, even one counter example being enough to throw doubt on Anselm's position? The many wonderful qualities you imagine when you think of a future partner may never actually be found to be the case in reality, where you might be disappointed.

- Many scholars hold that Kant has delivered a fatal blow to Descartes' OA, by his argument that going from the concept of God having **NECESSARY EXISTENCE** to God **EXISTING IN REALITY** is flawed and that existence cannot act as a predicate.

KEY QUOTES

1. *'I do not seek to understand that I believe, but I believe in order to understand'. Anselm*

2. *'From the fact that I cannot think of a mountain without a valley, it does not follow that a mountain and valley exist anywhere, but simply that a mountain and a valley, whether they exist or not, are mutually inseparable. But from the fact that I cannot think of God except as existing, it follows that existence is inseparable from God, and hence that he really exists'. Descartes*

3. *'Caterus put the point to Descartes that the OA doesn't demonstrate that God really exists. It only shows that the concept of existence is inseparable from the concept of God. Descartes' argument is only convincing for the claim that if God exists, God exists necessarily'. Lacewing*

4. *'It would be self-contradictory to posit a triangle and yet reject its three angles, but there is no contradiction in rejecting the triangle together with its three angles'. Kant*

5. *'The ontological argument is 'a charming joke''. Schopenhauer*

6. *'If God, a being greater than that which cannot be conceived,*

does not exist, then He cannot come into existence. For if He did, He would either have been caused to come into existence or have happened to come into existence, and in either case, He would be a limited being, which by our conception of Him, He is not. Since He cannot come into existence, if He does not exist, His existence is impossible. If He does exist, He cannot have come into existence…nor can He cease to exist, for nothing could cause Him to cease to exist nor could it just happen that He cease to exist. So, if God exists, His existence is necessary. Thus God's existence is either impossible or necessary. It can be the former only if the concept of such a being is self-contradictory or in some way logically absurd. Assuming that this is not so, if follows that He must necessarily exist'. Malcolm

CONFUSIONS TO AVOID

- "Gaunilo is an atheist"- not so. He believed in God but did not think Anselm's argument about the greatest possible being existing in reality as well as in the mind worked.

- Be very careful to know the differences between Anselm's first and second formulations, and then the difference between what Anselm is arguing and what Descartes (and even Malcolm, though he is not on the syllabus) is putting forward in their different ontological arguments.

- This is a topic that calls for **PRECISE DEFINITIONS** and these are perfectly possible if you pay attention to the different arguments that are being put forward. Learn and use technical terms, such as **A PRIORI, DEDUCTIVE, ANALYTIC** to demonstrate your knowledge of the argument, and then do put forward your response to the various scholars' views you have heard – you are expected to show personal and philosophical engagement with the arguments.

The Cosmological Argument for the Existence of God

KEY TERMS

- **COSMOLOGICAL ARGUMENT** - reasoning concerning the origins, nature and order of the cosmos.

- **INFINITE REGRESS** – in the cosmological argument, this refers to a chain of causes going back that has no beginning.

- **PHENOMENAL** – things which are perceived by the senses or by immediate experience.

- **DEDUCTION** - a type of reasoning whereby it is demonstrated that the conclusion necessarily follows from the premises (as seen in the Ontological argument).

- **INDUCTION** – a type of reasoning that takes specific instances and from them, draws a general conclusion (eg. as seen in the Cosmological argument).

- **A POSTERIORI** – knowledge gained after experience.

- **NECESSARY BEING** – a being whose non-existence is a contradiction.

- **CONTINGENT EXISTENCE** – something which, by its nature, does not necessarily have to exist, and could or could not have existence, eg you or me. Once existent, can go out of existence.

- **FALLACY** – an error in reasoning that renders an argument invalid or unsound, even when looking like it is logically plausible.

AQUINAS' COSMOLOGICAL ARGUMENT

The Cosmological Argument stands in contrast to the OA in that it is not deductive but **INDUCTIVE**. Aquinas put forward Five Ways for the existence of God, and the Cosmological Argument (CA) was outlined in the first three of those ways; Aquinas argued for the existence of God from **MOTION**, **CAUSE** and **NECESSITY** .

Aquinas commenced his argument with the **A POSTERIORI** evidence of the universe itself and asked why it existed (not just why there are things within the universe, but why there is a universe at all). Upon analysing such evidence, Aquinas noted that some things are in motion.   By motion, Aquinas meant the change that goes on in particular things within the universe, such as within a tree as it grows taller or sheds bark. (Note here that for Aquinas, following Aristotle, motion did not just mean physical movement, as something could be still and yet be changing, like the aforementioned tree).

For something to be in motion it must be, in Aquinas' words '**MOVED BY ANOTHER**' (something external to it). He gave an example of wood, which is changed/acted upon by fire to reach its potential of becoming hot. The change, Aquinas noted, could not be caused by the thing itself; something acted/moved to make the wood hot (fire), but then something moved to make the fire (friction) and so on.

Aquinas considered the possibility of this chain of motion going backwards infinitely (infinite regress) to get to an ultimate explanation for motion, but noted that this was not possible.

> 'There would then be no first mover, and, consequently, no subsequent mover, as subsequent movers move only insofar as they are moved by the first mover'. Aquinas

Aquinas, working from Aristotle, understood this first or prime, unmoved mover to be God.

Aquinas' second way is his argument from **FIRST CAUSE**. Nothing is its own efficient cause as it would 'have to exist prior to itself', which is impossible. Again, it is not possible to go back infinitely in the chain of causes as without a First Cause there would be no subsequent intermediate causes which would mean that there would be no present effects (things we see in place around us now). 'Plainly this is not the case', noted Aquinas, 'so we must admit a first efficient cause (itself uncaused) which everyone calls 'God.''

Aquinas' third way is based upon the idea of **NECESSITY** and **CONTINGENCY**. Contingent things are those things which could or could not be in existence, they are non-permanent; if they come into being, they go out of being. Because of that, 'it is impossible for them always to exist, for that which is possible not to be at some time does not exist. If everything is like that, at one time nothing existed.* If that were true, there would be nothing in existence now, because things only come to exist because of things already existing.'

Thus Aquinas posits the need for a necessary being whose necessity lies in itself because if everything was only contingent then there would be nothing today.

If there was a state of nothingness, which Aquinas argues would have been the case without one necessary thing, then **EX NIHILO NIHIL FIT**, (out of nothing, nothing comes), and yet there is something – so there must be something that has necessary existence. Things do not have to exist, but they do, and this could not be the case if everything was entirely contingent. The required necessary being is God, unmoved mover and first cause.

*As there is nothing necessary about their existence, given infinite time there would be a stage where nothing existed. Jackson very neatly suggests that if we added up the life-span of every contingent thing, we would never reach infinity, so there must be a time when nothing existed, if everything is contingent.

COPLESTON'S COSMOLOGICAL ARGUMENT AND RUSSELL'S RESPONSE

In 1948, a famous debate between **COPLESTON** and **RUSSELL** outlined key differences in understandings of any ultimate explanation for the universe. Copleston's argument from **CONTINGENCY** relied on the argument from Liebniz's **PRINCIPLE OF SUFFICIENT REASON**. Liebniz asked why there is something rather than nothing, which led him to look for an ultimate reason for the existence of the universe. He argued that there needs to be 'sufficient reason' to explain why something is the case. With regard to the existence of the universe, this sufficient reason cannot be given from the collection or sum of its constituent parts, as these are insufficient to explain the whole thing. The sufficient reason must be external to the universe because contingent things don't explain their own existence but are reliant on other contingent things.

This principle, and the way in which it is disputed, is central to the debate between Copleston and Russell. In summary, the argument went along the following lines:

- Copleston put forward the need for a **PRINCIPLE OF SUFFICIENT REASON** that is not found within the collection of contingent beings within the universe.

- Russell asked for clarification of such a principle, and wanted to know when precisely a sufficient reason is reached, and if sufficient reason for existence is the same as **CAUSE**.

Copleston noted that we can attribute cause to things that are contingent but that sufficient reason refers to a total explanation as to how the universe as a whole is in existence, not just those contingent things within it, which rely on being caused.

He stressed the inability of contingent things to provide their own sufficient reason; the reason for their existence must lie outside of them. If God is another contingent being, then he cannot have within him the complete reason for his own existence.

As a necessary (not contingent) being, God is his own sufficient cause.

Russell questioned the need for a sufficient reason, and whether such was possible anyway. He questioned if it is possible to go from contingent causes within the universe to a necessary sufficient and external reason, and wondered how such a move would be possible. Russell also said that necessary only applied to **ANALYTIC** statements such as a bachelor is an unmarried man, and saw no ground to talk of God as necessary.

Copleston responded by saying that just because a thing has not been found (the sufficient reason) it is not the same as saying it should not be looked for.

The contingent cause of events cannot provide a sufficient reason for the whole series; hence the need for a necessary being. He also suggested that Russell's unwillingness to enter the debate concerning a principle of sufficient reason is dogmatic; if a person refuses to come to the chessboard then a game cannot commence.

Russell maintained that the world 'just is'; it is **BRUTE FACT**. And that it is not possible to go from causes within the universe to a cause of the universe (famously saying that just because every human being has a mother, it does not mean the entire race has a mother). Here he is accusing Copleston of the **FALLACY OF COMPOSITION**, which assumes that what is true of parts must be true of the whole.

Copleston replied that God as a necessary being is not a first cause or mother as such, as that would mean God is another 'phenomenal' and contingent cause, which would not explain the whole series. God is an **ONTOLOGICAL NECESSITY**. Copleston went on to suggest that Russell was denying the reality of the problem regarding the existence of the universe by arguing it 'just is'. Which is right, Copleston or Russell here?

HUME'S CRITICISMS OF THE COSMOLOGICAL ARGUMENT:

Hume questioned why the world needs a first cause or a beginning. Why is infinite regress impossible? Even if we see cause and effect in the world (and Hume questioned this assumption), it does not mean that the universe itself be the effect of an uncaused cause, but the chain of causes could simply continue ad infinitum.

Furthermore, Hume famously challenged our understanding of cause and effect, noting that event a following event b does not meant that a caused b, even if we have not seen one instance when b did not happen after a. His argument noted that we put cause and effect together by habit rather than having any evidence that one caused the other. Hume's argument continues to carry much weight today and his questioning of cause has implications for Aquinas' claim that God is the first cause.

Hume questioned why there could not be more than one cause. The empirical evidence from the world gives no clues as to the number of causes that it required (if it required any), and, without being able to go outside the universe, Hume questioned how we would know if there was one or more causes. Maybe male and female Gods who are born and then die are more fitting from the empirical evidence we see in the world IF **EFFECTS RESEMBLE CAUSES** in any way – such Gods may fit the profile of the a posteriori evidence more closely than a Christian God. To stress, Hume, writing as an empiricist (and, remember, Aquinas is working from an a posteriori base), noted that we have no experience of the causer/s of the universe, which seems to be a unique case; we have experience of what we have called cause and effect within the world but how can we know about a cause outside the world; on what experience would we base such?

Hume questioned if the uniting together of different things within the universe and saying that 'the whole' has a cause is '**AN ARBITRARY ACT OF THE MIND**.' There is nothing in our experience, or any logical argument that can be made, to suggest that there is an overarching cause which gives a reason for the effects we see in the universe.

In response, Elizabeth **ANSCOMBE** has questioned Hume's argument about not being able to say that existence has not got a cause because we cannot go outside the universe to know that. She writes that it is possible to conclude that 'existence must have a cause' without knowing specifically 'that particular effects must have particular causes.' Whilst it is possible to imagine things coming into existence without a cause, this does not tell us if this is the case in reality.

STRENGTHS

- Could Aquinas' argument from causation actually tie together with scientific evidence of causation? Some scientists argue that Big Bang cosmology requires a causal factor. With the discovery of the Higgs Boson particle, the question still remains why such an important particle is in place. If we accept that we need to find an ultimate explanation or, as Leibniz stressed, a sufficient reason, do the arguments of Aquinas and Copleston still offer some useful ground?

- Is the discovery of effects without causes sufficient to fatally attack Aquinas' causation argument? Could it be that the cause of such effects has not yet been discovered rather than there not being a cause for them?

- The progress of science would cease if we took Russell's line 'things just are.' The developments we have seen are because we have attempted to answer the question, 'why are things the way they are?; what is the explanation in this and that case?' Perhaps Copleston was actually being more scientific in his quest for an answer to the whole series of events.

WEAKNESSES

- In the field of Quantum Mechanics, research is being carried out as to the idea of 'backward causation', and even the notion of uncaused events, and it is possible that our whole notion of what is meant by cause and effect will need to be re-evaluated. It may also be possible that matter or energy is eternal, and as such the necessary element of Aquinas' argument is not God but material itself. We can still ask, however, why that it is the case that matter has an eternal nature ('it just has' might be Russell's response, and this is an acceptable position for many).

- Does a cause that once existed have to exist today? Imagine someone who throws a model glider off the top of a cliff; the glider on its journey continues to move despite the person who threw it not being any longer involved in its ongoing motion and journey through the air. Does this mean the argument for God being the first cause has no relevance or importance anymore because his job has been completed, just as the thrower of the glider has completed her work? This argument does not understand what Aquinas was actually saying, as he was asking why there is **ANY MOVEMENT AT ALL**, rather than just proposing God as some kind of first pusher of a chain of events. For Aquinas, God is not the one who winds up the clockwork mouse and leaves it to run, but rather the one who is the necessary mover, the cause of all causes whose activity, unlike the one who winds up the mouse, has not ceased. God, for Aquinas, is the ultimate explanation for why there is cause or movement, the ultimate cause, without whom there is no ongoing universe, cause, movement or any contingent things.

- It is perhaps not difficult to understand that a string of contingent beings could always be in existence, overlapping in the time that they have being. This would mean, contrary to Aquinas' argument, that there never was a time when nothing existed, even from a contingent basis. Alternatively, could there be things which have always been in existence but will go out of existence at some time in the future?

- Does the universe need a 'sufficient reason', or is it, as Russell said, 'brute fact?' Is there a need for a cause outside of the world to explain its existence? Is there an overarching sufficient reason for existence? If so, why? But, is Russell's reply of 'brute fact', 'the universe just is', a very unphilosophical (almost anti-philosophical) approach which should not be encouraged in students?

- Does Copleston's cosmological argument suffer from the same difficulties that the ontological argument does when needing a Necessary Being for it to work? Whilst the concept of a necessary being might be possible, that does not make such a reality.

KEY QUOTES

1. *'The First-Cause argument rests on the assumption that every series must have a first term, which is false; for example, the series of proper fractions has no first term'. Russell*

2. *'To say that such a very complex and well-ordered universe comes into being without any cause or reason is equivalent to throwing one's hands up in the air and just saying that anything at all might happen, that it is hardly worth bothering to look for reasons at all. And that is the death of science'. Ward*

3. *Copleston argues that, 'the series has not a phenomenal cause but a transcendent cause,' to which Russell responds, 'that's always assuming that not only every particular thing in the world, but the world as a whole must have a cause. For that assumption I see no ground whatever'. Copleston replies:*

4. *'Well, the series of event is either caused or it's not caused. If it is caused, there must obviously be a cause outside the series. If it is not caused, then it's sufficient to itself, and if it's sufficient to itself, it is what I call necessary. But it can't be necessary since each member is contingent, and we've agreed that the total has no reality apart from its members, therefore it can't be necessary. Therefore it can't be uncaused;*

therefore it must have a cause'.

5. *'Though difficult, and still incomplete, there is no reason to believe that the greatest problem, how the universe came into being, and what it is, will not be solved; we can safely presume that the solution will be comprehensible to human minds. Moreover, that understanding will be achieved this side of the grave.' [ie the answer will be provided by science and not metaphysical reasoning or religion]. Atkins*

6. *'Not how the world is, but that it is, is the mystery.' Wittgenstein*

CONFUSIONS TO AVOID

The easy reply to Aquinas which is often given, which runs along the lines of, 'if everything needs a cause, what caused God?' is perhaps not the strongest one to make, in that it does not understand what Aquinas regards as cause or what he is suggesting we should understand God to be. God is not 'one other thing' or the first flicker of the line of dominoes, but the necessary unmoved cause on whom all other movement, change, cause and contingency is reliant.

Be very careful to understand and able to explain the **DIFFERENCES** between the Cosmological arguments of Aquinas and Copleston; they are related, but different and the use of Liebniz' Principle of Sufficient Reason will help you in your delineation of these differences.

The Teleological (Design) Argument for the Existence of God

KEY TERMS

- **TELEOLOGICAL** – telos refers to end or purpose, and whether, in this instance, there is an end purpose for which the universe is designed.

- **A POSTERIORI** – knowledge gained after experience; in this case, arguing from the experience of design and regularity in the universe to God.

- **ANALOGY** - where two things are compared as similar because they share common features (for example, a watchmaker designing and giving purpose to a watch and a world-maker designing and giving purpose to a world).

- **EMPIRICISM** – a position which holds that knowledge only comes through sensory experience.

- **DESIGN QUA REGULARITY** – design as it relates to regularity, in this case the regularity in the universe and how it works.

- **DESIGN QUA PURPOSE** – design as it relates to purpose, in this case the purpose for which things seem to be designed.

- **THEORY OF EVOLUTION THROUGH NATURAL SELECTION** – the theory accredited to Darwin which accounts for the survival of species through natural selection not design.

- **SCEPTIC** – a person who seeks to rigorously question, challenge and assess the evidence put forward within arguments which make knowledge claims.

Like the **COSMOLOGICAL ARGUMENT**, the Teleological Argument for the existence of God is an **A POSTERIORI** argument which attempts to show that the design, order, regularity and purpose of the universe infer the existence of a God who gives such characteristics to it. It is important to remember that the two teleological arguments studied were written before the theory of evolution through natural selection was articulated.

AQUINAS' TELEOLOGICAL ARGUMENT

AQUINAS put forward a form of the **TA** in the fifth of his Five Ways referred to earlier. This argument is often known as **DESIGN QUA REGULARITY**, (though you will also see it referred to as design qua purpose) which means design 'as relating to/pertaining to' regularity. The regularity refers to the order and pattern of things in the universe, such as the blossom that appears on trees regularly in the spring as if it was working to a pattern or order (many other examples from nature can be given).

In observing the world, Aquinas stated that objects which have no intelligence of their own function in an efficient way and achieve the best possible results.

This seems to be because they have been designed or directed to do so. He goes on to note, as a result of this observation:

> *'Things that lack knowledge cannot move purposely unless they are directed by some intelligent being: an arrow needs an archer*

to shoot it. Therefore there must exist some intelligent being who directs all things to the PURPOSE for which they exist. This being we call God.'

Just as the archer directs the arrow, Aquinas stated that God has given a direction to natural bodies, which have no rational powers to direct themselves, to enable them to reach their goal. There is an order and **REGULARITY** in nature seen in physical laws through which things reach their telos or end. This regularity and order is not produced by the objects themselves, or by chance, but has been given by an intelligent being, God.

PALEY'S TELEOLOGICAL ARGUMENT

PALEY's argument utilised design qua purpose as well as design qua regularity, and he made use of an analogy to draw conclusions about the nature of the world and the need for a designer who provides purpose and regularity. In this first part of his argument he was referring particularly to **DESIGN QUA PURPOSE**.

Paley asks the reader to imagine the scenario where someone bumps their foot on a stone as they are walking across a heath; on doing so, the person might not be drawn to ask where the stone came from as there is nothing particularly noticeable or special about it.

However, if the person was then to stumble across a pocket watch, (at the time a recent and impressive invention), they would immediately see that this object was more complex; within its mechanism a whole series of cogs and springs are seen to work together towards the aim of enabling the watch to tell the time. The observer might notice that it is due to the precise way in which the watch pieces were placed that the purpose of the watch is fulfilled, and there is a skill involved in placing these pieces together in exactly that order (and no other). From this, Paley notes that it is required that a **WATCH MAKER/DESIGNER** had put the complex mechanism together for its **SPECIFIC PURPOSE**.

From this basic premise of design, Paley moves on to the observation of the natural world, where much more complex elements such as the human eye work precisely together towards the purpose of seeing; the parts of the eye such as the cornea and the lens have to be put together in exactly the right manner to fulfil the purpose of seeing which suggests that a skilled designer, as in the case of the watch, is once again needed.

The intricacy and **CAREFUL ORDERING** of the design is far too precise for it to have come about that way by chance, and it does its job efficiently only because of that specific design which enables it to fulfil its purpose. Paley was fascinated by the natural world and used many other examples from nature, such as the precise number of teats on different animals which are suitable for the litter they have, to draw the conclusion that the giver of design qua purpose in the natural world is God.

Working against the backdrop of **NEWTONIAN PHYSICS** and the formulation of the laws of motion, Paley then went on to note how the universe also has an **ORDER** and **REGULARITY** to its movements, where it works according to predictable patterns which could not be generated by non-conscious objects. The precise order of planetary movement and the essential operation of gravity within specific natural laws, which lie within very narrow limits, impressed upon Paley how regularity is essential for life to take place on earth.

In a similar way to Aquinas, Paley drew the conclusion that such regularity and order is given by an external agent, God.

Paley is thus working from design, **A POSTERIORI** from effect to cause, using analogy to work with the idea that just as man-made objects, made for a purpose, require an intelligent designer, so the design in the universe requires an intelligent Designer; purpose and regularity in nature point to One who provides such.

Paley noted that his argument was not weakened if one had not seen a watch before; one would still infer a watch designer, and different conclusions would be drawn with regard to the source of the watch than that of the rock. Further, one did not need to understand how the watch was made, or how the parts work together. Paley even made note that at times the watch goes wrong, but that this did not invalidate the idea of it being designed. He also rejected the idea that it was the human mind that placed the idea of design upon the watch. These additional notes were implicitly addressing **HUME**'s criticisms of the argument from design.

CHALLENGES TO THE TELEOLOGICAL ARGUMENT FROM HUME, MILL AND DARWINISM

Hume

Whilst **HUME** pre-dated **PALEY**, he argued that the TA failed on several points. Hume was an **EMPIRICIST** and a **SCEPTIC**; an empiricist looks for observable evidence gained through sensory experience from which to attain any knowledge about the world, whilst a sceptic challenges arguments, and studies proposed evidence carefully before making judgement, realising the limitations of knowledge and the difficulty of reaching certainty. It is important that you bear this in mind as you go through Hume's challenges to the Teleological Argument.

Hume questioned the validity of Paley's **WATCH ANALOGY**. A watch works using strict mechanical movements, and Paley extrapolated from this that the world has similar hallmarks of design. Hume argued that this is not actually how the world 'looks'; it appears more organic in nature; it grows and develops on its own. Such things as cabbages and carrots are natural things, whereas the watch is not, which is why we pick it up and look at it carefully. Wilkinson and Campbell note that, 'by choosing a machine as our analogy, we have already determined the outcome we want.' For this reason, to go from arguing that a watch needs a watch maker and compare this to a world which needs a world maker is to use a flawed analogy.

The fact that evil exists in the world runs counter to Paley's claim that the designer is the God of **CLASSICAL THEISM** who is both all- good and all-powerful. Would such a God have created a world that exhibits evil? If God did design the world and leave it to run not only does the design he put in the world seem faulty and amoral but it hardly speaks of a personal and good God who is still interested in it. (Remember, Aquinas and Paley were not suggesting God was a disinterested Aristotelian Prime Mover).

Indeed, from the a posteriori evidence that Paley wants to use, it is very unclear that this would lead to posit an **INFINITE** God as creator, (as the world is finite), or a **PERFECT** God, (as the world is not perfect).

Hume suggested that such a world, if effects resemble causes, speaks more of an infant or inferior deity as its creator, a creator who was 'ashamed of his lame performance.'

Such a designer might also no longer be alive.

Hume asks how it is possible to arrive at the idea of ONE **DESIGNER** of the universe from the evidence we have. Even the watch might involve several designers, such as the designers of the springs and the cogs. If apparently straightforward things within the world require a team of designers, is it not just as feasible, if Paley wants to retain the use of his analogy, that a team of designers, each with different skills, were required to design the universe? Paley might respond that God has all skills, but then this is a faith statement rather than an outcome directly derived from his watch-maker analogy.

Hume noted that we have **EXPERIENCE** of seeing how machines or houses are made, but do not have this for the designing of a universe. Therefore, how can we possibly know that this world was designed without being able to step outside the world to see such a process, as we can do when we observe the designing of a house? Using such experience we legitimately note that such design was due to an architect. And even seeing order in the universe does not suggest an order giver; how, indeed, would we know this world is ordered if we have no other world with which to compare it?

If the **INTRICATE COMPLEXITY** of the world requires an intelligent designer, then why doesn't an intelligent mind require a designer, and so on, and so on? Hume wondered why we would stop at God when seeking an explanation for intelligent design.

Although pre-dating Darwin, Hume argued that there could be many other ways to explain apparent design, including the idea that in an infinite universe this particular world could be the one where a stable combination of atoms (Hume would not have used that word) enabled this world to arise. Hume is here working with an understanding of the universe known as the **EPICUREAN HYPOTHESIS**, in which it was argued that natural forces gradually form into order from chaos. An analogy is that, given enough time, monkeys left with a typewriter would type out a Shakespearean sonnet; this would not, however, be through intelligent aforethought, but randomly as one of many possibilities which, given time, would happen. Where stability is evident, **PALEY** has read design, order and purpose given by a designer, but Hume argued that such a leap is not inferred at all as there are other explanations for such order; simply put, if it were chaotic then the world would not have survived.

Responses to Hume

Is he correct to say, when questioning Paley's analogy, that different things, such as watches and worlds, cannot be compared? It is common practice to extract similarities between very different types of objects (for example, principles of flight in an insect and a helicopter). Does Paley's comparison of design in both the watch and the world thus stand?

Swinburne has criticised Hume for suggesting the possibility of a multitude of creators as going against **OCKHAM'S RAZOR**, where the explanation with the fewer unnecessary complications is to be preferred when arguments are being compared.

FLEW has questioned the 'monkeys typing out a Shakespearean sonnet' analogy as completely unfounded and not a comparison that can be used with the multitudinous factors that have to come together in a precise fashion for this world to form. He argues that following where the evidence leads from the complexity of the universe suggests an intelligent designer as the more probable and plausible explanation (rather than a proof).

Mill

The natural world is unbearably cruel and violent and animals do things which if they were human they would be tried for; things such as certain animals giving their prey a lingering and agonising death hardly gives evidence of a creator who is wise and all-loving when creating and designing. **NATURE** itself, through its inbuilt processes like earthquakes and hurricanes, causes untold misery and destruction. This argument is formed after the publication of **DARWIN's** Origin of Species and takes note of the harsh, remorseless and unsympathetic way in which species die out if they do not adapt to the environment.

As Mill, like Hume, was an **EMPIRICIST**, he evaluated the evidence of the world before him and noted that, if there was a creator, then he certainly was not the God suggested by classical theism. It could not be deduced from a world that contains barbaric evil that God was all-knowing, all-loving and all-powerful, just or, indeed, worthy of worship. Such a maker seems to not just allow but will suffering. In support of Mill, **DAWKINS** argues that God must be a sadist who enjoys spectator sports if the same God made the tiger and the lamb, the cheetah and the gazelle.

Responses to Mill

Is nature 'cruel' or just natural? Is 'cruel' a human interpretation of events that are simply part of survival? Does an earthquake have 'thought' about its effects, and are these natural processes actually both necessary and 'good' for enabling human life to survive (if human life is seen as a 'good' thing)? **MILL** might respond by saying that it really takes a particularly distorted view to call such atrocities in nature good.

The theory of evolution through natural selection states that those species whose **MUTATIONS** fail to suit their environment die out, and the genes of those who were able to survive are passed on (be careful though, as Darwin did not know that genes were passed on or of **DNA**). It is therefore not design that enables a certain species to survive, but evolution which operates 'blind', working along the lines of 'survival of the fittest'.

Dawkins argues that it is DNA that controls the destiny of a species, including human beings, and not the other way round, and this applies to every life form on earth.

Apparent design, such as strong beaks on birds, are actually just features of those birds who have had mutations within their genes and benefitted from the stronger beaks which enables them to get the food that birds with weaker beaks could not crack open. Those with such strong beaks then survive and reproduce, passing on the strong beak genes. Those birds whose genes undergo other random mutations, ones that do not help the bird survive, mean that such birds just die out, and so we are left with what might look like design as birds have the beaks they need. But birds without those beaks would simply no longer be in existence. This argument does follow the principle of Ockham's Razor as it does not infer any external agent of whom we have no evidence.

Beneficial changes aid efficiency and therefore secure survival. Whilst the operation of certain species looks quite complex due to many minute natural changes and countless adaptations over time, this is not to be confused with **DESIGN FOR PURPOSE** given by an external agent. There is no overriding purposeful design to elements within the universe, or any overriding pattern or regulated plan that joins the whole thing together; evolution is not heading anywhere. Homo sapiens and other species are those creatures who have had the mutations that have adapted them to this current environment - survival is the only 'driver', but this is not governed by any external force or design agent.

Humans are, however, a species that have 'progressed' or mutated into exhibiting rationality, which runs counter to the idea of Genesis, that man has fallen from a higher state of grace to a lower state of sin.

Responses to Darwin

Although the process of evolution has been called blind, it is still possible to ask if the process as a whole has some element of design given to it. How is it that the world is so organised that evolution can take place? Has God placed the very precise natural laws within the world which allow evolution to occur? With increased knowledge of the universe as a whole, it has become evident that the conditions which support life have to be very precisely ordered and a single minute factor different to the ones in place would not have resulted in the possibility of life or evolution. **DAWKINS** and **RUSSELL** might respond that this is the world just 'as it is', and we only know that this is the world we have because we have evolved to tell the story.

STRENGTHS

- We can think of **NATURAL LAWS** that Aquinas would not have known in any scientific detail, such as gravity, and agree that they do work according to a regular pattern so that bricks do not fly upwards when dropped. Is his reading of the regularity in nature correct to the extent that we question things when they seem not to follow a pattern or regularity?

- As our knowledge of the **INTRICACY** of the universe grows, and how millions of factors have to be very precise for the earth, let alone human life, to exist as it does, would this support Paley's argument that there seems to be design and regularity? Although writing at a time of great scientific advance, during which the world was increasingly viewed mechanistically, neither Hume nor Paley would have had access to today's scientific data regarding the fine-tuned precision of the universe. Would this support Paley's argument?

- Does evolution through natural selection provide sufficient **REASON** to explain the universe as a whole? Does it still require an instigator/designer? Do very precise conditions within the universe, which allow for the process of evolution to take place, simply arise by chance? In any other field where such finely tuned conditions come together we might say that someone has made sure those precise systems have been placed together at certain temperatures and distances; would chance be a poor scientific response in that case? Is science being true to itself by suggesting evolution happens naturally, or is it valid to still look for the reason why evolution takes place?

WEAKNESSES

- As a general point it is worth asking if everything serves a purpose, or the best purpose, on every occasion? Is purpose placed on things by human observers?

- Going from a watch, which cannot be produced by natural means, to the natural world and saying that both give evidence of external design might not actually be valid. Whilst a watch infers an external designer, natural things can be produced by natural means. It could be argued that there is design within the natural order, but this does not necessarily mean that such design was given from an external agent in the way the watch received its design. The shared inference breaks down because it cannot be shown that the natural objects have to have an external design in the way in which the fabricated watch demonstrates.

- How strong are the traditional teleological arguments now that the theory of evolution through natural selection has much scientific evidence with which to support the idea that natural adaptation explains apparent signs of design? Hume might still say that we have no way of knowing that evolution is the explanation rather than design, but, as an empiricist, he might say that it provides stronger probability.

KEY QUOTES

1. *'If Aquinas had lived today, he would doubtless have argued that the evolutionary hypothesis supports rather than invalidates the conclusion of the argument…[and that it] clearly points to an extrinsic intelligent author of [non-intelligent material], who operates for a purpose'.* Copleston

2. *'The way in which living things work, which requires a huge coordination of lots of tiny bits, each doing their specific job, is amazingly complex. This coordination, the detail and intricacy of interrelations between parts, suggests planning – a plan that follows a purpose….Acting on a plan guided by a purpose is design. It's as if someone had in mind that the eye should see, and put the bits together to ensure that it could. The way living creatures are suggests they are designed…..If living creatures are designed, then as a matter of definition, there must be a designer. You can't have a design without a designer'.* Lacewing. (Be careful not to say that this is Lacewing's personal view – it may or may not be; it is the way in which he sets up the exploration of the design argument).

3. *The parts of the watch are 'put together for a purpose, eg, they are so formed and adjusted as to produce motion, and that motion so regulated as to point out the hour of the*

day...... Every indication of contrivance, every manifestation of design, which existed in the watch, exists in the works of nature [and those] contrivances of nature surpass the contrivance of art, in the complexity, subtlety, and curiosity of the mechanism'. Paley

4. *For stars to form, the 'initial strength of the explosion in the Big Bang had to be precise to one part in 10 to the power of 60. That's as precise as hitting a one-inch target at the other side of the observable universe.... Science cannot explain why the Big Bang was exactly the size of why the laws of nature are the way they are.... one obvious explanation is that the Big Bang, the properties of matter-energy, the laws of nature, were all designed to allow life to evolve'. Lacewing*

5. *'There is a danger of turning the argument from design on its head. Human arms were not divinely designed to be at the exact level of door-handles – it was the other way round. Hen's eggs are not providentially planned to fit exactly into egg-cups – it is the other way round'. Richards*

6. *'In a universe of blind physical forces and genetic replication, some people are going to get hurt, other people are going to get lucky, and you won't find any rhyme or reason in it, nor any justice. The universe we observe has precisely the properties we should expect if there is, at bottom, no design,*

no purpose, no evil and no good, nothing but blind pitiless indifference'. Dawkins

7. *'Everything, in short, which the worst men commit either against life or property is perpetrated on a larger scale by natural agents'. Mill*

8. *'We find it hard to look at anything without wondering what it is 'for', what the motive for it is, or the purpose behind it.' [But we should not read] 'malevolent purpose into what is actually bad luck'. Dawkins*

9. *'Many of the questions religion tries to answer are not real questions…..the question concerning the purpose of the universe is, an entirely invented question'. Atkins in Taylor*

10. *'The only watchmaker in nature is the blind force of physics'. Dawkins*

CONFUSIONS TO AVOID

- Do not suggest Mill was arguing that the world was not designed. Although he might well have thought that it wasn't, the thrust of his argument was that the evidence simply did not suggest that the designer of the world was all-good, all-powerful, all-knowing and just, as the Judeao-Christian tradition, including Aquinas and Paley, believed.

- Darwin's work did not set out to attack the design argument. Whilst Darwin realised that the consequences of his theory were that the world as science was now beginning to understand it did not require a designer, he remained agnostic, and other factors in his life, such as the death of his daughter, and exposure to other religions on his travels, had bearing on his own faith position. See the Science and Religion section for more on this.

Kant's Moral Argument

KEY TERMS

- **POSTULATE** – something implied or asserted to find a solution to a dilemma, which is probable but not provable.

- **GATEGORICAL IMPERATIVE** – an unconditional and universal moral principle that is based on duty rather than any outcome that might come from its operation.

- **AUTONOMY** – the freedom of will to make decisions.

- **THE SUMMUM BONUM** – the highest good; the state where happiness and moral virtue come together.

- **DUTY** – the obligation to carry out an action because it is intrinsically right, in this case, the good will.

- **A PRIORI** – knowledge gained prior to experience.

- **A PRIORI SYNTHETIC** – the moral law within is a priori, before experience, but its working out requires practical verification in the world of experience, and is thus synthetic.

- **THE EGO, THE SUPEREGO, THE ID** – elements in Freud's model of the mind.

KANT'S MORAL ARGUMENT

Necessary background:

It is essential to realise that Kant is not suggesting that his moral argument is a **PROOF** for God; in fact 'argument' is not really the correct term to use. He did not think proving the existence of God was possible, as this goes beyond human experience, and so rejected traditional arguments for God's existence. In fact, Kant's moral argument for God is central to his **ETHICAL THEORY**, which is studied in the other half of the AS course, and must be understood as the framework in which his postulate for God works.

Kant's moral argument rests on postulates, which are not proofs. A **POSTULATE** is something implied or asserted which is **PROBABLE** but not provable. This will become clear as we go through Kant's moral argument. For Kant, God is as a postulate of practical reason who guarantees the **SUMMUM BONUM**. His moral argument points to the probability that God exists because God is the solution to how the summum bonum, which is the rational requirement of a moral universe, will be realised; if the summum bonum is not realised at some point then we live in an irrational universe, which goes against what the moral law suggests.

HOW THE ARGUMENT WORKS:

Kant worked from the foundational premise that the universe is **FAIR** and **RATIONAL**, though he admitted that this could not be proved. However, it is suggested by the existence of an **INNATE AWARENESS** of a moral law within each person. By moral law, Kant meant that, **A PRIORI**, every person has a powerful sense of right and wrong, though not always the knowledge of how to act. In saying this, Kant, in a bold move, was claiming that morality is **A PRIORI SYNTHETIC**; whilst we have a moral law, we need knowledge gained through experience of the world in order to verify the rightness of our moral actions.

In such a rational universe, morally correct actions would lead to the state of the highest good, **THE SUMMUM BONUM**. This would be the state where virtue and happiness combine.

How can the moral law work so that the summum bonum operates? Kant answers, by each person doing their duty, which is to act according to the good will. The good will is that which is good in itself and is action that does not look at personal benefit but carries out moral requirements according to **DEONTOLOGICAL, CATEGORICAL MAXIMS** and not by looking towards **TELEOLOGICAL, HYPOTHETICAL** outcomes. This means that a person always treats another person as an end not a means to an end; and this categorical imperative applies universally (in a rational universe).

If the moral law within suggests that we ought to do our duty and carry out the good will, then it should, according to reason, be possible for us to do this. It would be irrational otherwise. Therefore we must be free agents – **AUTONOMOUS** - and able to freely rise above the supposed 'masters' of human nature, pain and pleasure. **AUTONOMY** is a postulate of practical reason put forward by Kant; that is, something that cannot be proven but is likely to be the case to provide a resolution to a problem. Freedom allows us to fulfil the duty that the moral law suggests; we are enabled to move from 'ought' to do our duty to 'can'.

People who do their duty in acting according to the **GOOD WILL** and who thus follow categorical maxims, clearly do not see the summum bonum realised, as they are just as likely to face disaster or end up unhappy; likewise, those who are clearly immoral seem to get away with things. It seems from the evidence that it is not within our powers to bring this state about because, as Kant notes, we are not the 'cause of the world and of nature itself' and we could not guarantee anyway that happiness would follow even if the moral law was universally fulfilled. How can this be in a **RATIONAL UNIVERSE**? Either the universe is not rational, which Kant rejects, or there is somewhere where the summum bonum takes place and someone who brings that about. Someone brings together, in a **NECESSARY CONNECTION**, virtue and happiness.

As a result of the above reasoning, Kant argues that in a rational universe, it is necessary to postulate **IMMORTALITY** as the place where the summum bonum occurs, and God as the guarantor that it will occur.

The moral law in a rational universe leads to God.

Kant distinctly wants to move away from other moral arguments where God is the giver of the moral law through **CONSCIENCE**. (See chart). Where, previous to the move of the Enlightenment, faith took central place, man's **REASON** is the starting point which leads, through the moral law and the summum bonum, to postulate the existence of God. We are **INNATELY** aware of this moral law and framework of the universe. This innate awareness indicates the summum bonum is rational and right. Though not the motive, the summum bonum is the result.

The chart helps track the development of Kant's argument. It is read from the bottom up:

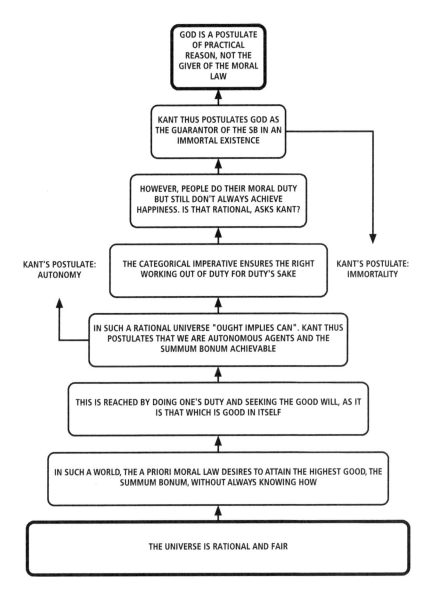

PSYCHOLOGICAL CHALLENGES FROM FREUD

FREUD did not believe that there was any reason to postulate a divine guarantor of the highest good or any objective moral law. Rather, through his analysis of the human psyche he argued that morality developed internally in the process of **UPBRINGING** and in reaction to societal pressures.

Through his work in the area of neurosis, Freud found that a person's interactions with parents had an enormous impact upon the formation of a person's moral sense. As a child, we are driven by the part of the mind called the **ID**, which is the name Freud gave to our **INSTINCTUAL DRIVES** and self-centred desires. As we grow, we quickly come to feel a sense of **GUILT** that our desires, and, in particular our sexual desires and the desire for our mother, are restricted. This development results in the formation of the **EGO**, which is the part of our **PSYCHE** which takes account of the realities of how the world is, and is shaped by external influences, traumas and early experiences. The ego helps us to interact with society. It is the part of the mind of which we are most aware as it is our conscious self.

Freud then went on to argue, from his psychoanalytic work, that what he called the **SUPEREGO** develops from the ego. This superego internally watches over the ego like a policeman or parent and punishes the ego with feelings of guilt and anger when it reminds the ego of the restraints and behaviour required by society. Within the superego, humans reason and make decisions and, in this way, the superego is similar to the **CONSCIENCE**.

To stress, as this relates directly to the issue of our moral sense, our conscience stems from the superego in the unconscious mind, and acts to restrain our actions with a **SENSE OF GUILT**. This 'inner parent' punishes and rewards us when we either disobey or act in accordance with the superego. Furthermore, Freud argued that the unconscious 'id' also influences us, as it stores unconscious desires and basic instincts, which can sometimes surface in dreams and under hypnosis.

Here we can clearly see that his internal explanation of moral awareness is a very different explanation for morality than that which **KANT** offers. For Freud, any moral sense of what is right and wrong within the psyche comes from a combination of our parents and society and the pressures upon us from these sources and our internalised reactions to them, not from reason. Its source is, ultimately, **PSYCHOLOGICAL**.

We **INTERNALISE** the instructions that influential authority figures give us and any 'internal voice' that develops is purely a product of the superego element of the psyche and not reason's reaction to an objective Kantian moral law. A further difference is that any moral sense is not headed towards a summum bonum guaranteed by God, but is shaped by influences and pressures on the psyche as we respond to a reward and punishment that corresponds to our experiences of when we do right and wrong.

Furthermore, Freud went on to argue that religion itself is a **NEUROSIS** which enables people to feel that their needs are being met and their desires for consolation and hope satisfied. A relationship with a Father-figure to replace our own father, and the promise of an afterlife, are both very attractive and could help us stop being too disturbed when things don't go well in life. By challenging this idea, Freud adds a further challenge to Kant's claims. As **TAYLOR** notes,

'The summum bonum being achievable is a very persuasive human desire, but this is no way makes it or God, as the postulate of pure reason, a reality.'

It is important here to realise that not only the question of the source of morality is questioned by Freud, but the 'source' of God also. Kant's moral argument might arrive at the need to postulate God, but Freud's alternative explanation is of the creation of a God by us, formalised by man-made religion, and this God fulfils our desires, particularly for a Father-figure. This is a way in which Freud's argument from **DESIRE** can be used to critique Kant's postulate of God from the basis of **REASON**. **LACEWING** suggests that this can be looked at both ways however: is God the creation of human psychology or does the human psyche have spiritual needs because God creates us like that?

STRENGTHS

- Perhaps there is an **INNATE MORAL SENSE** that there should be a summum bonum, where right action combines with happiness, and it is to this that Kant appeals. It could be argued that there is a strong sense of the need for moral fairness within humanity, whether or not we believe that there is an ultimate place where the highest good happens. Universal declarations of the moral worth of a human being and the quest for justice which treats everyone with equal dignity might suggest Kant's argument has some grounding in human experience.

- Kant commences his moral argument with an appeal to **REASON**. This immediately allows people who do not believe that there is a God, and who would not agree that God is the source of morality, to at least allow Kant some ground at that stage of his argument. They would not draw the same conclusions that Kant does concerning God as the guarantee of the summum bonum (or even that there is a greatest good), but the fact that they might be prompted to reflect on reason and whether the universe is fair, might be an attractive feature of Kant's argument.

- In response to Freud, it could be argued that, whilst a sense of guilt and the formation of the superego form the basis of our morality, this does not explain why such a sense should arise. It could be that, just as Kant's claim that the universe is fair is an assertion, Freud is equally guilty of asserting an unprovable claim. Is his declaration that the superego is developed in the psyche in response to society's pressures, putting forward something that cannot be proved?

WEAKNESSES

- Davies has questioned Kant on the postulate of God as guarantor of the summum bonum, asking why it would necessarily require a God to fulfil this role. Could it not be, he asks, a **'PANTHEON OF ANGELS'** or a being who simply has the power to bring about such a state?

- Are there alternative and more valid arguments concerning the source of morality? These could include **SOCIETAL NORMS** which, through the process of evolution, humanity has worked out according to the community environment in which they live and wish to survive. These norms include mutual respect, laws of justice and punishment and the balance between serving the needs of self and those of others. Is there need to go beyond this to a God?

- Is there any justification in saying that the summum bonum

NECESSARILY has to come about? Hick has argued that whilst 'ought implies can' is logically consistent, this does not mean that such a state exists, or has to exist, in reality. A student ought to aim for an A grade in Philosophy and Ethics, but this does not mean they have failed or their effort regarded as meaningless if they do not reach it. If the summum bonum does not have to exist, does God have to be postulated as its guarantor? The claim that a moral impulse pushes everyone towards aiming for the highest good can also be questioned by the evidence that many people settle for less than the highest good.

- Is the universe **RATIONAL** and fair as Kant claims? Whilst many would say it should be, this is not the same as saying it is. Perhaps life is 'nasty, brutish and short', or at the least have no overarching point, and the hope of a summum bonum is a pipe dream. If we do not accept the universe is fair and rational, does the rest of Kant's argument work? And therefore how useful is it as an argument that leads to postulate the existence of God?

CONCERNING FREUD

Many of Freud's claims from psychoanalysis have been disputed, not least because of the limited amount of empirical evidence and case studies he himself produced to support his theory. The emphasis Freud placed on **SEXUAL TRAUMA** as the source of neurosis is also strongly disputed. **POPPER** has dismissed Freud's psychology as a pseudo-science because Freud's claims can never be falsified and every human predicament fits neatly into his scheme. What Popper means by this is that if an adult says, 'I have a problem relating to women', Freud would say that is because of early childhood experiences. If another person said, 'I have no problem relating to women' again Freud would say that such is because of their early childhood experiences, and Popper argues that, because it is so 'wide' a theory, its claims can never be falsified and as a result it ends up saying nothing; as such it is not actually a science. (Popper's falsification is studied at A2). These criticisms might undermine the strength of Freud's claim for an alternative source of morality as stemming from the psyche.

KEY QUOTES

1. *'Have the courage to use your own reason – that is the motto of enlightenment'. Kant*

2. *'Kant's view was not that morality is pointless unless there is a God to reward it. Things are right and wrong per se, in Kant's view, and therefore he concludes that there must be a God'. Ahluwalia*

3. *'I cannot think of any need in childhood as strong as the need for a father's protection.........at bottom, God is nothing more than an exalted father'. Freud*

4. *'It would be very nice if there were a God who created the world and was a benevolent providence, and if there were a moral order in the universe and an after-life; but it is a very striking fact that all this is exactly as we are bound to wish it to be'. Freud*

5. *'Freud [can] be criticised for setting out to find a theory which supported his view, rather than forming his view on the basis of evidence....he took for granted Feuerbach's PROJECTION idea and worked from that, with an assumption from the outset that there is no objective God. It is therefore hardly surprising that he comes to the conclusion that religion is false, as this was also his starting point'.* Ahluwalia*

*Of course, it could be argued that Kant also starts with the assumption that the universe is fair and rational and then likewise sets out to 'find a theory which supported his view.'

CONFUSIONS TO AVOID

- "The Summum Bonum is the motivating factor for good action". Not true, as the Summum Bonum, or highest good, is part of **REASONED REFLECTION** by each person, and is not some immortal goal that spurs us on to moral action. Rather, we act towards the highest good when we act morally, so, as Thompson says, we 'make it a reality by responding morally.' It is not, as Thompson goes on to say, 'something 'out there', an ideal we have to believe in before we can act morally.' Neither should you say that Kant is trying to prove the existence of God; his reasoning is more subtle than that.

- Be careful to note that philosophical and psychological theories do not arise in historical vacuums. How much was Kant influenced by his family's Lutheran **PIETIST** background? Does this background mean that, ultimately, though the source of morality will be the innate moral law, his theory will inevitably lead to God? Is it possible to say that Freud's negative experience with religion had no influence upon the formation of his theory concerning the God-less source of conscience, morality and neurosis? This is contentious ground, and one that students rarely refer to; it is not something that should take up a lot of time in an exam answer, but could be a useful critique of moral theories. When we are looking for sources of morality, or at least whether morality points to the probability of a God or not, it could just be useful to take note of the wider context in which these theories are formed. We can at least ask if scholars can arrive at a conclusion on where our morality comes from that isn't somehow informed and influenced by the historical setting in which they write and which they are influenced by. (See second **AHLUWALIA** in key quotes). Does this diminish the usefulness of their claims, or is it just an inevitable part of any theory?

Challenges to Religious Belief: the Problem of Evil

KEY TERMS

- **THEODICY** – literally, theos (God), diké (justice); an attempt to justify the existence of God in the face of the existence of evil and suffering. In particular the attempt to defend the existence of a God with the attributes of omnipotence and omnibenevolence.

- **MORAL EVIL** – intentional actions by humans which cause suffering.

- **NATURAL EVIL** – events in nature which result in suffering.

- **OMNIPOTENT** – literally 'all power'; God having the characteristic of being all powerful.

- **OMNISCIENT** – literally 'all knowledge'; God knowing all things, including future events.

- **OMNIBENEVOLENT** – literally 'all good'; God, a being who is all good or loving.

- **PRIVATIO BONI** - the privation of good; evil is not a substance or entity but the privation, or lack, of good.

- **EPISTEMIC DISTANCE** – distance from knowledge of God.

- **ESCHATOLOGICAL** – normally referring to the end times, or the end of history; in Hick's theory it refers to post-death.

The arguments studied so far may have seemed very theoretical and not always related to the reality of our existence. The challenge to the belief in a good and powerful God which is presented here is far more personal and relates to the sometimes painful and anguished EXPERIENCE of being alive and aware that there is suffering in the world. However, whilst this is true and the argument concerns real and evidential evil and suffering, do not let emotion cloud your responses to this issue.

WHAT DO WE MEAN BY EVIL?

Scholars have classically divided evil into two types, though in reality there are many links between these types and the distinction between the two is not always easy to delineate (for example, think about an event such as a flood following heavy rain; this would seem like a natural event, but might actually have been caused, or made much worse, by deforestation carried out by man). The two types are:

- **MORAL EVIL** - This term is used to denote evil actions committed by human beings, such as rape, murder and war as well as actions which result in psychological and mental pain. These actions are freely committed and result in suffering, sometimes on a mass scale. There are countless accounts of atrocities that show the depth of human cruelty, including modern day examples.

- **NATURAL EVIL** - This term refers to events in nature that cause suffering, and which are not directly the result of human action, such as earthquakes and hurricanes. There are countless examples of the devastation that natural events cause, where thousands of lives are lost and habitats destroyed in a very short space of time. Disease and illness would also come under the title of natural evil. Philosophers disagree as to whether such 'natural' events should be called 'evil'.

The issue at stake in this argument is the challenge such events present to the belief in a good and powerful God, who is not only held to have created the world with such regular and devastating natural disasters, illnesses and diseases present in it but who seems to allow such to continue to take place.

THE PROBLEM

- If God is all-good he would not allow moral and natural evil to exist. Having a **BENEVOLENT** nature, he would have the motivation to abolish evil.

- If God was all-powerful, he would be able to stop evil. Having an **OMNIPOTENT** nature, he would have the ability to eliminate it entirely.

- And yet **EVIL EXISTS**.

Within the Judaeo-Christian tradition, God is also believed to be **OMNISCIENT** (although this is often included as an element of omnipotence). Omniscience raises further issues because it would infer that God knows that evil is going to happen but does not prevent it from doing so. The subject studied earlier in this guide concerning the nature of God as the **CREATOR** is also relevant here; if God created everything in the universe ex nihilo then the question needs to be asked if God created evil.

Earlier arguments concerning whether the universe has an ultimate purpose and meaning also come into play. A **THEODICY** attempts to reach a 'big picture' conclusion about a reason why things exist (including the possibility of a 'purpose' for the existence of evil), whereas many think such a search for overarching reason and meaning is both futile and unnecessary. Indeed, Russell finds the idea of the world as accident more plausible than the world as a **PURPOSEFUL** work of a God.

On the evidence of the immense amount of suffering in the world, Russell states that the most fitting description of God, if he existed, would be 'a fiend.'

A key question is how can an all-loving and all-powerful God tolerate one incident of suffering in his creation? Is there a solution to this problem which maintains God's character as understood in classical Theism even in the face of evil, or, as **HUME** suggests, does one of these attributes of God have to be removed to solve the inconsistency?

The attempt to justify the existence of God in the face of evil and suffering is called a **THEODICY**. Whilst some scholars such as **RUBENSTEIN** say that it is impossible to frame a theodicy after the horrors of Auschwitz, those that are formulated normally attempt to:

- blame a source other than God for the existence of evil, or

- say why evil is justified or even necessary for a greater good, or

- reinterpret (without removing) what is meant by omnibenevolence and omnipotence.

Few theodicies take the line that evil does not exist, (they cease to be theodicies if they did) but AUGUSTINE does conclude that evil is not a substance as such, as explained below.

THE THEODICY OF AUGUSTINE

AUGUSTINE'S THEODICY continues to have influence upon Christian thought, fifteen centuries after it was written. We can take his argument step by step:

Augustine's opening premise was that God, who is perfect, and therefore all-powerful and all-loving, made a good world. He based this understanding on the teaching of **GENESIS**, where God declared that his creation was good at the end of each of the first five days and very good at the end of the sixth. The universe, with a **HIERARCHY OF BEINGS** from God down to angels, humans and the rest of creation was ordered and in harmony.

However, after the creation of a good universe, both angels and man fell. The **FALL OF ADAM AND EVE** is outlined in Genesis chapter 3. Augustine argued that they clearly **FREELY CHOSE TO DISOBEY GOD**. They chose not to do what is good and rejected what God had told them to do and in so doing chose 'non-being' material things rather than the fullness of their being, God. Hence, by their **ORIGINAL SIN** of disobedience to God's instructions, Adam and Eve introduced a break and discord between them and their creator, God. Humanity **FELL** from a close relationship with God.

This 'choosing' of evil', was actually choosing to not live up to the standard of goodness that God intended; because it was choosing not to do that which is good, it is a **PRIVATION**. By this, Augustine meant that **EVIL IS THE LACK OF GOODNESS**, like blindness is the lack of sight. To stress, evil, in Augustine's theodicy, is not a **SUBSTANCE**, but the lack of good. In Latin, the phrase is **PRIVATIO BONI**. We can think about this idea of privation using many examples - cold is the absence of heat, ill health the absence of health etc. - and these things only have understanding in relation to what they lack. Adam and Eve now lack 'right order' and harmony with God - they have chosen to be **DEPRIVED**.

The idea of '**LACK**' is very important, but be careful. It is not evil that a stone lacks the ability to talk, or a worm lacks the ability to walk. These are qualities that the stone and the worm lack, but because they lack them they are not evil. However, when man chooses to not 'hit the mark' (this is what 'to sin' means), he is evil in the sense that he fails to live up to his morally good and God-given nature. And the choice to do this is due to our **FREE WILL** and hence, carries with it **RESPONSIBILITY**. If someone cannot use their arm due to an accident, they lack the health of the arm, but they cannot help this, unlike the lack of kindness we show when we are cruel to someone. On this point **TAYLOR** writes,

> 'According to Augustine's view, if you say that a human being is evil, or that their actions are evil, you are saying that the way they behave does not match expectations about how a human being should behave. For example, if you racially abuse people, rob or torture them, you are not living up to the standards expected of human beings. It is the failure to be what you should be that is wrong.'

Evil therefore comes about because of Adam and Eve's **FREE MORAL CHOICE**. Adam and Eve, when tempted by **LUCIFER**, use their free will to not live to the standards for which they were created, and through this disobedience, evil enters the world; as noted, evil here is not as a substance in itself, but the lack of goodness. Both moral and natural evil stem from the wrong moral choices made. Pain in child-birth and hard work making the soil productive are both immediate results listed in **GENESIS 3**. **MORAL EVIL** comes through Adam and Eve's choice, which sets them at a distance from God; **NATURAL EVIL** is due to the balance of nature being upset and the work of the fallen angel **LUCIFER**, who tries to be more powerful than God, bringing discord to nature which results in suffering. But, **AUGUSTINE** argued that free will is a good thing in itself as it enables good and right choices to be made and is worth the price of evil occurring. Of course, if God is perfect, he would have known humanity would make a wrong choice and fall, but he chose for humans to have free will so that they could freely love him rather than be robots without choice.

AUGUSTINE argued that the goodness of the world is seen clearly when people choose to do good as it stands in contrast to when people do evil and misuse their free will, just as 'a dash of black makes the colours in a painting stand out' (**PHELAN**). This is known as the **AESTHETIC PRINCIPLE**; as Augustine writes:

> *'In the universe, even that which is called evil, when it is regulated and put in its own place, only enhances our admiration of the good; for we enjoy and value the good more when we compare it with the evil.'*

God did not create anything **IMPERFECT**; he could not therefore have created evil. Thus, evil is not a 'thing'. Neither is God in a **BATTLE** between the forces of good and evil – spiritual forces at war might make people not responsible for their choices, and **AUGUSTINE** stressed human responsibility stemmed from humans being free to choose. But be careful not to say that Augustine denied that evil existed; it 'exists' not as a separate 'thing', because God would have had to have made it if it was a thing, but evil exists as a **LACK OF GOODNESS**. Indeed, later

Augustine goes on to say that evil comes from God due to the fact that he keeps human beings in existence, and they are beings who have this free choice to become evil.

Now Augustine has established that Adam and Eve's choice gives birth to evil, how does he account for ongoing evil in the world? As all humanity is descended from Adam and Eve, then all humans inherit their **SINFUL NATURE**, which chooses to live in rebellion towards, and in discord with, God, and not reach the standard for which God created us. Augustine says that humans are **'SEMINALLY PRESENT'** in Adam, and, as such, our punishment is deserved.

For Augustine, 'all evil is either sin or punishment for sin'.

However, Christ is the **'SECOND ADAM'** who shows God's grace and mercy in offering humanity a chance to restore its relationship with God and avert hell, which would be just punishment for sin.

Key steps:

1. Creation is perfect; God is all-powerful and all-loving.

2. Adam and Eve have free choice - a good thing.

3. They, and Satan, freely chose not to do good - **PRIVATIO BONI** (the Fall). God does not create evil.

4. Humans and angels are responsible for this choice which brings moral and natural evil into the world, resulting in suffering.

5. The goodness in the world as a whole can clearly be seen when contrasted with when people choose the privatio boni. God keeps in existence people who have freedom to choose not to be good.

6. The sinful nature of Adam is present in humans.

7. Jesus offers a way for human nature to be restored.

STRENGTHS

- It could be argued that the default position of humanity is good, in that we are offended when people do harm; news reports are full of things which go against our expectations, such as murder and conflict, and this is why they are news. Is this a hint that the world is 'good', as Augustine suggested, and that evil is a privation of that goodness? Do we feel that the world is 'out of balance', which is why there are so many attempts to help those who are less fortunate than ourselves or who suffer through the effects of natural disasters? Is this better than any evolutionary explanation there might be for trying to preserve the weak?

- The idea of **EVIL LACKING SUBSTANCE** can make **LOGICAL SENSE**, just like darkness being the absence of light and cold the absence of heat are logically coherent ideas. **LAW** has recently challenged this idea however, and said that from the clues in the universe, God might in fact be evil; such a God just puts some good in the world to let people think he is good. He argues that the idea that 'God is evil' can be supported from the world with as much credence as the idea that 'God is good.'

- If **FREEDOM AND RESPONSIBILITY** is to be genuine, then our choices have to have consequences, otherwise it does not matter what we choose to do. It has been argued that this is the type of freedom we seem to experience and which is at the heart of **AUGUSTINE's** theodicy. The alternative to unrestricted moral freedom seems to suggest something less than what it means to be human.

- The idea of freedom and interpretation of the ideas at the heart of Augustine's theodicy does not depend on a **LITERAL** reading of Genesis. Many Christians regard the meaning found in the Genesis story of moral and natural evil reflecting an accurate reading of the human condition and humanity's free response towards God and how we act in creation.

WEAKNESSES

- Does our **EXPERIENCE** agree with the idea that evil is simply the lack of good? To those who have been victims of rape or violence, or genocide on a mass scale, there seems to be more than the **PRIVATIO BONI** at work. It does not seem that the careful planning, organisation and implementation of shockingly cruel and depraved acts which were part of the Holocaust can be explained by thousands of people just lacking the good.

- Does Augustine's theory explain **WHY** angels and humans should choose to not obey God? It would seem that this even stumped Augustine; concerning why the will should be turned not to do the right thing, he said, somewhat surprisingly, 'let no one, then, seek to know from me what I know that I do not know'.

- Giedrius **SAULYTIS** writes that according to Augustine, 'to seek the causes of this defection is as if someone sought to see darkness, or hear silence. Thus, the problem of evil is wrapped up in mystery', other than that created things, 'have within them the tendency toward non-existence' (which is to choose against their good and become corrupted and deprived).

- If Augustine does not know the **ULTIMATE CAUSE AND REASON FOR EVIL** and why humanity wills to do it, of what use is his theodicy as an explanation?

- Following on from the above point, God's goodness can be questioned if the whole system is set up in a way that allows for such suffering on a massive scale. Schleiermacher has pointed out the **LOGICAL CONTRADICTION** in the idea that a perfect world could go wrong. And how could such a world go wrong if there was no knowledge of evil for humanity to choose at the Fall?

- Despite the offer of God's grace in the form of Christ, is it a loving God who keeps a system going in which every successive generation after Adam (including, for Augustine, babies) is punished for original sin? Not only is this a problem as far as the **JUST NATURE** of God is concerned, but biologically each human being is not descended from Adam. That being the case, in what sense can the idea that we are 'seminally present in the loins of Adam' work? Scientific understanding would also question the whole underlying source of Augustine's theodicy, including Adam and Eve and an **ACTUAL FALL** of man, which, despite claims otherwise, might still require a literal reading of Genesis. **EVOLUTION** through natural selection over time to the stage of rational human beings, lies in contrast to the Genesis reading which starts with a perfect world and a humanity that falls away from a blissful state.

- Many, such as **DOSTOYEVSKY**, have questioned the idea of a loving God based on the sheer amount of suffering in the world, even if it allows humans to be free; is God's loving gift of freedom worth this cost? It would be difficult to quantify how much suffering is too much; should toothache not be allowed for example? Others have questioned how a good God could conceive of the existence of a punishment such as **HELL**.

THE THEODICY OF IRENAEUS

While Augustine's theodicy is sometimes called a **SOUL-DECIDING THEODICY**, as we choose/decide what we will do with the good gift of free will, **IRENAEUS'** argument is known as a **SOUL-MAKING THEODICY**. It has within it a very different idea of the source of evil. Writing two hundred years before Augustine, Irenaeus' theodicy works in the following way:

1. Irenaeus read the **GENESIS** creation account **LITERALLY**. From this basis he argued that God desires for humanity to reach **PERFECTION**, but that this perfection is something to be reached from an initial state of imperfection (this is different to Augustine's belief of humans falling away from perfection). Humans are created **IMMATURE**, but can progress towards maturity and perfection. Irenaeus worked with the teaching of **GENESIS 1** verse 26, where humans were made in the '**IMAGE**' of God, but were to develop into the '**LIKENESS**' of God.

2. It is important to unpack this idea. **COLE** notes that this is a move from the 'form' (image) of God to the content (likeness) of God. The Good News translation of the bible uses the words 'they (people) will be like us (God) and resemble us.' **TAYLOR** et al note that Irenaeus understands 'like us' as God creating people with 'intelligence, morality and a personality' and the state of 'resembling' God as peoples' souls growing 'until they resembled the very nature of God.'

3. Being child-like, humans make **MISTAKES** and do things which are not wise, but this is a result of both their lack of maturity and the **FREEDOM** they have. In Genesis chapter 3, Adam and Eve

are exiled, (through an actual event known as the Fall), from the Garden of Eden to make the journey towards God's likeness in a world which is suited for them to make such a pilgrimage. Whilst they do bear some responsibility for their choices against God's commands, **IRENAEUS** held that the serpent who tricked them is to blame. Adam and Eve are banished from the garden, but this is not punishment in the Augustine sense; **TAYLOR** notes that such punishment is offered in the way children are set boundaries, and it is therefore 'educative.' Neither is the Fall as catastrophic for **IRENAEUS** as it is for **AUGUSTINE** as it is a mistake which is part of the human experience of growing up, rather than a movement away from perfection, and there certainly is no sense of '**ORIGINAL SIN**' in Irenaeus' theodicy, unlike there is in Augustine's.

4. In the playground of this world, humanity can develop, and grow towards 'good.' Evil and suffering provide **TESTS** for that growth but humans can make moral progress in the world as they journey. Irenaeus noted that in the bible there were many people, such as **JONAH**, who went through suffering in order to grow, make mistakes, learn the need to repent and fulfil the purposes God had for them. How we react to this suffering is the key. And **JESUS**, through suffering, restores the damage that Adam has done by his choice and makes it possible for there to be union between God and man again. Jesus rescues those taken captive by the serpent by taking Adam's sin on the cross, restoring friendship between God and man.

Thus, **EVIL IS NECESSARY** as an essential part of the environment in which humanity can grow, in which we can choose to live above our basic animal instincts. God, who is all-good and all-powerful, allows evil and suffering as part of the environment in which the journey from imperfection to perfection takes place and therefore there is purpose for both good and evil within the creation of the universe. (This is very different to **AUGUSTINE**'s explanation of evil). Evil and suffering are necessary in order to help us develop **MORAL VIRTUE** and maturity, to grow in character to resemble God, and be good like him, eventually achieving perfection. Without suffering and the prospect of death, there is no testing which provides opportunity for growth and repentance and learning of what is good; neither would there be any contrast between what is good and what is evil (see the aesthetic principle). For Irenaeus evil is not a privation, but a very real and necessary part of the world in which we develop towards maturity. As **AHLUWALIA** writes, 'evil was necessarily for the existence of good'. If so, does this offer a possible philosophical answer to the problem of evil?

Because the world is like this, it is what **HICK** calls, a '**VALE OF SOUL-MAKING**'. Our souls can choose to live towards ourselves or towards God, to develop kindness and empathy and to learn from our mistakes. Being created perfect would not have given us the opportunity to develop and learn. This growth requires a determination of the will within the reality that the choices we make with our free will have consequences. Expecting to be bailed out every time we make an error would not develop our souls and compromise genuine free will.

The journey **CONTINUES AFTER DEATH** because the soul carries on its journey until ready to enter heaven; it is important, however, to note that for Irenaeus those who continue to reject God and who do not grow will face punishment post-death.

HICK has developed Irenaeus' ideas to argue that humanity is able to make this evolutionary journey towards a relationship with God. He argues that in this world humanity is at an **EPISTEMIC DISTANCE** from God, meaning, at a distance of knowing God, and can, through free choice, make a journey towards God, developing goodness in the face of a world which contains evil and disasters. The world seems to be one which is entirely suited to enable soul-making to go on. Indeed, our **RESPONSE** to catastrophic events can potentially help to **DEVELOP CHARACTER** traits such as empathy, kindness and compassion. Humans have the knowledge of the laws of nature in which they can explore the world, but it is precisely those predictable and regular **LAWS OF NATURE** which govern the fact that earthquakes and hurricanes exist, or bricks remain hard (and do not suddenly by some divine intervention become soft) when they fall on someone's head. In addition to this, because of the fact that we are truly free, we can cause suffering, or have pain inflicted on us. **HICK** argues that without the possibility of these dangers, **NO PROGRESS WOULD BE MADE** either within the soul of a person or in any area of life such as the arts or the sciences, and in a world of no suffering, nothing actually would ever be seen as right or wrong. No real virtues would develop when we act kindly without the possibility of us not choosing this path and acting maliciously.

This process through suffering makes the soul (although you could argue that for **DOSTOYEVSKY** this very process crushes the soul). Hick differs from Irenaeus by suggesting that eventually everyone will be able to enter into a relationship with God post-death as only **UNIVERSAL SALVATION**, which completes the making of everyone's soul, fully satisfies the purpose of God allowing evil and suffering in this world. Because Hick suggests that the pain of this world has an ultimate answer post-death, his approach is **ESCHATOLOGICAL**.

THE FREE WILL DEFENCE

Central to the theodicies of **AUGUSTINE, IRENAEUS** and **HICK** is the idea that there has to be evil and suffering in the world if humans are to be genuinely free; we have to have **THE POSSIBILITY OF CHOOSING WRONG**, with the **REAL CONSEQUENCES** of those choices, in order for us to be **TRULY FREE**.

For Augustine, the choice made when humanity misused free will resulted in evil which is taken on the cross by Christ. For Irenaeus the free will to choose is part of our soul's development towards the likeness of God.

Is this freedom worth the cost? What are the alternatives? **MACKIE** suggests that God could have made a world in which humans always choose what is good, but many have rejected this as not what is meant by freedom. Others have suggested that perhaps our choices could result in less suffering than they seem to in this world. Others question whether a God of love should have made such a world at all.

STRENGTHS

- Does part of what it means to be human and **GENUINELY FREE**, necessarily involve the possibility of choosing good and evil? Irenaeus argued that for a person to have any less a choice would mean he is no longer human. What would it mean for human identity if freedom wasn't genuine and there wasn't good and bad choices to be made?

- Could the development of humanity really have happened **WITHOUT RISK** or danger or difficulty? Would virtuous choices develop if we did not have **ALTERNATIVE CHOICES** that we could make? Would we progress if God intervened all the time rather than letting us learn from our mistakes? Is it better and **MORE LOVING** parenting to set boundaries (laws of nature), but allow freedom within those boundaries and encourage (rather than dictate) good choices? Do we sometimes work on the principle that some suffering is indeed worth the end result? If so, is it possible to translate that principle to a cosmic level?

- **POST-DEATH** resolution of the problem of suffering might indeed be a way of fulfilling God's purpose for people to move from being in God's image to his likeness. It would suggest that for those who suffer unimaginable pain in this life, the whole journey is **NOT FUTILE**, which, if this life was all there was, it might seem to be. Is it possible to offer alternative hope if there is no life after death?

WEAKNESSES

- It is difficult to understand why there needs to be the **EXTREME AMOUNT** of suffering in the world for humans to learn. After a certain amount of pain, the human soul might actually fail to learn its lesson. For children born into extreme poverty, involving malnutrition, to suggest the idea of suffering as a soul-making journey could seem almost immoral. If, further to that, such children are to continue their journey of soul-making in the afterlife (what does this mean - that they would suffer further, post-death, in order to learn and develop more?), would this seem fair or loving in any way? In reference to this idea, suffering seems to be so randomly allocated.

- **PHILLIPS** questions how a **GOD OF LOVE** can **JUSTIFY SUFFERING** to fulfil his purposes. He is particularly critical of viewing a kind response to the suffering of others as a way of developing one's soul; it would almost suggest that people should look for the suffering of others and, in a way, be grateful for it as it gives them a chance to respond kindly and develop their character. Using suffering as a means to justify the end (**INSTRUMENTALISM**) of moral development is an example of a case where a theodicy adds to the problem of evil rather than solves it. Could there be alternative pain-free ways to develop the soul?

- How strong and philosophically valid is any theory that relies on post-death existence for its solution? Is the theodicy more likely to be accepted on **THEOLOGICAL** grounds by a believer than **PHILOSOPHICAL** grounds by an atheist?

FURTHER CONSIDERATIONS

AUGUSTINE tried to move away from the idea of evil being 'God's fault,' whilst Irenaeus argued that evil could serve a purpose. In general, when writing about the 'fault' idea, students should be careful. It could be useful to hold the 'God's fault' argument in **BALANCE**. If God is blamed when an earthquake takes place, is it logical to thank him when one doesn't? If God is blamed for seemingly faulty features of the universe, is it consistent to thank him for beauty and laws of nature that mean, for example, trees grow and produce fruit? What would Augustine and **IRENAEUS** say about the 'balance of blame and thanks?'

How does one classify illnesses such as cancer? If cancer occurs as a direct result of smoking, is **GOD** to be held **RESPONSIBLE** for the very possibility of the occurrence of cancer in the person, or is the smoker responsible for misusing their freedom, knowing the possible consequences? Could there be a world in which we could do what we like without bad side effects or would this not be what we mean by human existence? Is God's **OMNIPOTENCE** limited by logical possibilities, so that this type of world would be a logical contradiction, or, as **DESCARTES** argued, does God's omnipotence mean that he must be able to do anything and not be limited to what is logically possible? **BRAND** has written extensively on the idea that pain is God's gift to the world as without its use as a barrier on our actions, we would suffer even more. Further, he notes that the same sensitivity that withdraws fingers when placed on something sharp is precisely the same preciseness of touch needed to play the piano softly. However, **HEBBLETHWAITE**, in **AHLUWALIA**, writes:

> 'Part of the problem of evil is the fact that, the structure of our
> bodies, nerves and brains being what it is, physical and

mental torture (as well as disease and accident) can take such horrific forms.'

What would Augustine and Irenaeus say to these ideas?

Does God's foreknowledge of the fall of man and subsequent evil make **GOD ULTIMATELY RESPONSIBLE** for it in Augustine's theodicy? Did God not have the power to make humans not able to sin, if he could see that we would? Augustine says,

> *"God indeed had the power to make humans who could not sin. But He preferred to make them so that they had the power to sin or not sin as they wished. As a result there would be humans who gained merit from not sinning in this life and who received in the next the reward of not being able to sin"* (see SAULYTIS).

Augustine seems to be saying that creating human beings able to sin is not the same as 'they will sin,' and having free will and the possible disastrous consequences of that is better than not having free will. But does this still make God responsible if he knew humanity would choose to use their free will for evil? Augustine responds by saying that humans are not compelled to sin by external factors, like a stone has no choice but to fall when dropped. **MORAL EVIL**, unlike the stone's fall, is a **VOLUNTARY** use of free will. Even though God's knowledge is perfect and must include knowledge of the fall of man, humans freely make choices. Augustine thinks God's omniscience and human freedom are compatible. Is this convincing? These questions are studied further at A2.

KEY QUOTES

1. *'Either God cannot abolish evil, or He will not; if He cannot, then He is not all-powerful; if He will not, then He is not all-good'. Augustine*

2. *'That which is the evil of all things in which any evil is perceptible is corruption. So the corruption of the educated mind is ignorance: the corruption of the just mind, injustice; the corruption of the brave mind, cowardice. In a living body the corruption of health is pain and disease'. Augustine*

3. *'According to Augustine there was no evil in creation before angelic and human sin. It came into existence when first angels, and then humans misused their wills turning from their creator'. Saulytis*

4. *'God must have been on leave during the Holocaust'. Wiesenthal*

5. *'God judged it better to bring good out of evil than to suffer no evil to exist'. Augustine*

6. *'The glory of God is the human person fully alive'. Irenaeus*

7. *'A world which is to be a person-making environment cannot be a pain-free paradise but must contain challenges and*

dangers, with real possibilities of many kinds and disaster, and the pain and suffering which they bring'. Hick

8. *'In a world devoid both of dangers to be avoided and rewards to be won we may assume that there would have been virtually no moral development of the human intellect and imagination, and hence of either the sciences or the arts, and hence of human civilisation or culture'. Hick*

9. *'Never shall I forget that night, the first night in camp, which has turned my life into one long night, seven times cursed and seven times sealed....Never shall I forget those moments which murdered my God and my soul and turned my dreams to dust.' (Elie Wiesel's harrowing autobiographical story of his survival in Auschwitz acts as a first-hand account of the evil of which man is capable, and should be read for an understanding of what is meant by 'moral evil' at its worst, and how such made Wiesel think deeply about God, evil and humanity).*

10. *'Many have argued that there is a contradiction involved in the fact of evil and the belief in an omnipotent all-loving God. However, it does not seem logically contradictory, since it is not the same as saying, 'there is a God and there is no God.' It is not logically necessary that an omnipotent all-loving God prevents evil, and a theodicy is an attempt at a solution of the*

problem of evil, without denying God's omnipotence or love
or the reality of evil. It shows God is justified in allowing evil'.
Cole

11. *'Imagine that it is you yourself who are erecting the edifice of*
    human destiny with the aim of making men happy in the end,
    of giving them peace and contentment at last, but that to do
    that it is absolutely necessary, and indeed quite inevitable, to
    torture to death only one tiny creature, the little girl who beat
    her breast with her little fist, and to found the edifice on her
    unavenged tears – would you consent to be the architect on
    those conditions?' Dostoyevsky

CONFUSIONS TO AVOID

- Note that the theodicies are put forward to defend the existence of a God who has certain characteristics. To simply say that the existence of evil in the world means it is impossible to believe in God is not what this topic is about. **ARISTOTLE'S PRIME MOVER** type God has nothing to do with the world and therefore the existence of suffering would not at all be an argument against such a God, as the Prime Mover is never once declared as loving or interested in humanity. Be careful to note that theodicies are trying to justify why a **POWERFUL AND LOVING GOD** allows evil.

- Highlight the differences between **AUGUSTINE** and **IRENAEUS**, as their theodicies differ in many ways. Be very clear that you are aware of their explanations of the source of natural and moral evil, the role of free will, the purpose of evil and the ongoing effect of evil in the world. If you do use Hick's development of Irenaeus, make sure you say that that is what you are doing.

Challenges to Religious Belief: Religion and Science

KEY TERMS

- **CREATIONISM** – a theological position in which the creation accounts of Genesis are read literally and given higher authority than scientific theories of the creation of the universe and evolution.

- **THE BIG BANG THEORY** – a scientific theory which holds that time, space, matter and energy arise from a point of singularity that inflates to form the universe.

- **DARWINISM** – the theory of evolution by natural selection.

- **INTELLIGENT DESIGN** – the idea that the universe shows signs of intelligent design, and this is a better explanation than undirected random changes that result in complex systems in nature.

- **IRREDUCIBLE COMPLEXITY** – some systems in nature, such as certain cell structures, have parts within them that are co-dependent and could not evolve by small independent changes. Such interdependent complexity requires an intelligent designer.

- **NON-OVERLAPPING MAGISTERIA** – separate fields of experience and authority, such as science and religion, do not overlap; science and religion have different concerns and ask different questions.

SCIENTIFIC VIEWS ON THE CREATION OF THE UNIVERSE

THOMPSON gives clear definition to the meaning of both science and religion when he writes: Science is, 'the systematic examination of the world using experimental methods to determine physical laws and principles in order to explain the way things are.' Religion is, 'an attempt to give an overall view of the nature of life, to explain why things happen, and to influence events, through the help of a God or Gods or through the acting out of moral principles.'

With such descriptions as background, the following questions are raised:

1. Is it possible to maintain belief in God in the light of scientific understandings about the origins of the universe and human life?

2. In view of current scientific knowledge, what 'solution/s' to the questions concerning the origins of the universe are the most rational and satisfactory, and can issues surrounding why anything exists be explained without recourse to God?

3. Can scientific hypotheses and explanations, such as the Big Bang theory, and religious belief be held together, or is it inevitable, as some argue, that the former invalidates the latter?

4. Are religion and science fundamentally different, and possibly complimentary disciplines, which attempt to answer different questions using different methods?   The latter idea was described by **GOULD** as 'non-overlapping Magisteria' (see key terms), though it is questionable whether science and religion neatly remain within their Magisteria.

COSMOLOGY AND THE BIG BANG

COSMOLOGY concerns questions about the origins of the universe. The Big Bang is a relatively modern, and the most widely accepted, scientific theory which seeks to give an explanation of origins. It states that:

1. There was a beginning to the universe, which came from a **'SINGULARITY'** around 12-14 billion years ago. Singularities are thought to exist at the core of black holes and are areas of intense gravitational pressure in which, 'finite matter is actually squished into infinite density.' The universe begins as 'an infinitesimally small, infinitely hot, infinitely dense singularity'.

2. For some reason, this singularity inflated (**THE BIG BANG** - although it's better thought of as an inflation rather than an explosion), and matter and energy originated from it. Literally, nothing existed – space, time, matter, energy – before the **SINGULARITY** (space appeared inside the singularity, not the other way round). Over billions of years, expansion and cooling takes place to form the size and temperature of the universe.

3. Over time, while expansion is still taking place, stars and planets form.

DOES THE BIG BANG GET RID OF GOD?

Whilst physicists such as **GENTRY** have questioned the traditional model of the Big Bang as a proposed explanation for the beginnings of the universe, it remains the most popular scientific theory.

The key question for this topic is if science adequately explains why the universe exists and if it does so without need for God.

If it is argued that the Big Bang acts as a **SUFFICIENT REASON** for the existence of the universe, then no external agent is needed to bring this about. It could be that the universe is, as Taylor notes, 'self-explanatory', because science and scientific laws explain why the universe comes into existence. Scientists, perhaps most noticeably **DAWKINS** and **ATKINS**, note that, whilst there is no **GRAND UNIFIED THEORY** at present that acts as an all-encompassing explanation for the existence of the universe, it is **SCIENCE** that will eventually achieve such without need to make reference to God. **HAWKING** thinks we can ditch the God hypothesis and reference to ancient creation myths completely.

Others note that the above might be a **CIRCULAR ARGUMENT**, and does not explain why such precise physical laws exist to bring about a universe. Among others, **WARD, FLEW** and **SWINBURNE** have come to the conclusion that an **EXTERNAL AGENT** is a much more valid and simple explanation for the origin and order of the universe. Taking the Genesis creation accounts **NON-LITERALLY**, and holding these stories as myths - stories given for a moral and 'value' purpose - allows insights from within both the religious and scientific fields to be held together and **COMPLIMENTARILY**.

There is no need for the theist to deny science and scientific theory under this view; those who take this position, such as **POLKINGHORNE**, argue that a satisfactory and sufficient reason for precise and coherent scientific laws in creating the conditions under which the Big Bang takes place is the existence of an **ABSOLUTE EXPLANATION**, that being an eternal being. The most suitable hypothesis for why anything exists and why, when it does, such existence is governed by physical laws, is God. This, theists would note, is a much more **REASONABLE** explanation than the argument that the universe, and the minutely precise laws and long and complex sequence of events required to make it possible, is either **SELF-EXPLANATORY** or comes about **BY CHANCE**. Whilst self-explanation begs the question, the extreme unlikeliness of this event (added to the fact that conscious life arises) makes the proposal of chance as the sufficient reason a less adequate solution than that of a being of intelligence. Some theists argue that **GOD IS THE GRAND UNIFYING THEORY**, rather than a being that, conveniently but rather unconvincingly, can be inserted into the gaps when science is unable to explain things.

An atheist might reply by suggesting that it is only because we are here that we are able to argue about this matter, as the conditions of the universe about which we are disagreeing are obviously the ones that have resulted in human life, and so the dice has rolled in the manner which allows the discussion to take place. But that does not mean there needs to be a 'dice-roller', just that, 'we are here' and if we were not our existence would not be something about which we could be arguing.

The latter position is a **WEAK** version of the **ANTHROPIC ARGUMENT**, which says that if the world were different we would not be here, but there was nothing saying that it had to be this way. A **STRONG** version of the anthropic argument, put forward originally by **TENNANT**, suggests that the world had to be made this way for the development of human life to take place; the precise events that result in human existence are so unlikely to have come about randomly that there is good reason to suggest a guiding hand who accurately finely-tuned (and tunes) the universe and all its conditions for human habitation.

CREATIONISM

Whilst there are many different 'types' of creationist models, ranging from Gap Creationism to Old Age Creationism, the central distinguishing feature of creationism is the belief that the account of creation in Genesis is factually and historically accurate and that this account is to be held in higher regard than a scientific theory, especially if the latter contradicts the Biblical record. Genesis is an accurate account of the origins of the universe, because it is given by God, **WITHOUT ERROR**, to humanity, and **GOD ALONE** was at creation. Creationists do not agree with the positions outlined above which combine religious and scientific views.

The example of creationism most at odds with the Big Bang account of origins, which dates the universe as billions of years old, is **YOUNG EARTH CREATIONISM**. With a **LITERAL** reading of Genesis, this position holds that God created the entire cosmos in six twenty-four hour days between 6,000 and 10,000 years ago. Young Earth Creationists also believe that a literal flood made possible the quick laying down of strata and fossils within it.

Other creationists allow for an **OLDER DATING** of the universe, where God is the creator of the Big Bang – the 'light' referred to in the creation story. Within this strand of creationism, each 'day' is interpreted as an era in which the earth develops, though **MORRIS**, a 20th Century creationist, completely rejected such an interpretation of the word day as era, finding no possible compromise between a belief in the Bible and evolution. As can be seen, it is important to realise that when writing about Creationism, this approach involves a '**WORLDVIEW**' and not just a belief about specific events – a worldview that regards science as secondary to the Bible in every aspect.

Obviously, the challenges here revolve around how an ancient text can be taken literally in the light of scientific findings. There are problems with this view, not least of which is the notion of whether a 'pure' reading of the Bible is ever possible anyway, as even translation of the Hebrew text to English involves some interpretation. Others have argued that it was not written with the intention of being read literally, but this does not remove its truth value if truth is conveyed in more ways than 'fact'. In addition to these **THEOLOGICAL** difficulties, there are many **SCIENTIFIC** problems raised against creationism, such as the **FOSSIL RECORD**, the **AGE OF GEOLOGICAL FORMATIONS** and the results of **CARBON-DATING**, which, many evolutionary scientists argue, is strong evidence that even planet earth itself is over 4.5 billion years old.

DARWINISM AND VARIOUS DEVELOPMENTS OF EVOLUTIONARY THEORY

Darwin's theory of evolution by natural selection, and some of Dawkin's response to the idea of design in the universe, are outlined in the chapter concerning the teleological argument for the existence of God. Following the publication of Darwin's **ORIGIN OF SPECIES**, some theologians within the Church, who did not read Genesis literally, did not see evolution as challenging core beliefs. However, others argued strongly that such a theory denigrated the Biblical image of man. Such debate must be read in historical context, which was one where the Church held enormous sway and many scientists were clergymen, which might have influenced their findings.

The most famous debate at that time was between **WILBERFORCE** and

HUXLEY, in which Wilberforce challenged the gaps in Darwin's theory and the idea that 'species, although variant, were fixed and fundamentally stable' (**AHLUWALIA**). The crucial question at the time was if Darwin's theory meant the need to abandon faith in the Biblical account of **MAN'S UNIQUE PLACE AND THE DEVELOPMENT OF SPECIES** in creation. Darwin's theory suggested that evolution was the process by which change took place rather than a God who fixed species and provided variety in creation; it also made hints that man was not at all unique, but simply part of the long evolutionary line. **AHLUWALIA** notes the reaction to the debates at the time:

> 'Some abandoned religious faith as superstition; some tried to find ways of compromising; others rejected the possibility that the theory of evolution could be right, and maintained their believe in the literal truth of biblical accounts of the origins of humanity.'

RICHARDS adds that, 'others survived by living two different lives on weekdays and Sundays.'

Developments in recent years have taken a form which draw **ATHEISTIC** conclusions from Darwin's theory. **DAWKINS** and **DENNETT**, among others, argue that natural selection **INEVITABLY** involves taking an atheistic view of the universe, as the overwhelming evidence for evolution through natural selection completely explains the variety found within nature today. It is useful to question if this is true to Darwin's own position. To quote at length from Darwin's personal correspondence:

> 'With respect to the theological view of the question; this is always painful to me.— I am bewildered.— I had no intention

to write atheistically. But I own that I cannot see, as plainly as others do, & as I should wish to do, evidence of design & beneficence on all sides of us. There seems to me too much misery in the world. I cannot persuade myself that a beneficent & omnipotent God would have designedly created the Ichneumonidae; with the express intention of their feeding within the living bodies of caterpillars, or that a cat should play with mice. Not believing this, I see no necessity in the belief that the eye was expressly designed. On the other hand I cannot anyhow be contented to view this wonderful universe & especially the nature of man, & to conclude that everything is the result of brute force. I am inclined to look at everything as resulting from designed laws, with the details, whether good or bad, left to the working out of what we may call chance. Not that this notion at all satisfies me. I feel most deeply that the whole subject is too profound for the human intellect. A dog might as well speculate on the mind of Newton.— Let each man hope & believe what he can.—

Certainly I agree with you that my views are not at all necessarily atheistical. The lightning kills a man, whether a good one or bad one, owing to the excessively complex action of natural laws,— a child (who may turn out an idiot) is born by action of even more complex laws,—and I can see no reason, why a man, or other animal, may not have been aboriginally produced by other laws; & that all these laws may have been expressly designed by

an omniscient Creator, who foresaw every future event &
consequence. But the more I think the more bewildered I
become; as indeed I have probably shown by this letter.

The current debate between the truth and implications of evolution versus Biblical creation accounts has found its most virulent expression in North America, and has sometimes centred on the idea of an either/or approach. **EITHER** you believe in science OR religion; for many religious believers, the two, and particularly belief in evolution, cannot be combined because:

The cold and indifferent process of evolution undermines the **UNIQUE STATUS OF HUMAN BEINGS** as the crown of creation who displays, alone among creation, the image of God. It devalues man as an evolved chimpanzee, which is different to the Biblical picture of a unique creature set apart from the animal kingdom

GOD CREATED SPECIES AS THEY ARE. God, who is perfect, (as opposed to scientific theory) creates species as they are and they do not mutate, though some creationists believe that life can adapt within species; to support this view they argue that the fossil record of change from one species to another is lacking.

If evolution is correct, there is death and pain in the natural order before man and woman are on the scene; taking a **LITERAL** reading of Genesis means that sin, pain, suffering and death, only come into the world after the creation of humanity.

It should be noted here that literal readings of the Bible and the view that God specifically created humanity versus scientific accounts of the Big Bang giving birth to the evolutionary process lead to **DIFFERENT UNDERSTANDINGS OF THE HUMAN BEING, THE SELF AND**

EVEN PURPOSE. It should be clear that these differing accounts of creation and the arrival of man on the world's scene have significant bearing on current understandings of human nature, and are not just interesting differences about how life began and develops.

However, this irreconcilable approach between religion and science, most on evidence during the **1925 TRIAL OF JOHN SCOPES** (of which you should be aware) is a very recent development. For centuries the scientist saw himself as attempting to solve the mysteries of God's world. Today, many within religious traditions, and some scientists who hold a religious faith, have been able to combine science and religion by arguing that God has created the very precise natural laws in which the opportunity for evolution occurs and God provides an ultimate explanation for existence itself. Whilst **DAWKIN**'s atheism means a rejection of Biblical accounts, **WARD** also rejects a literal reading of creation but maintains faith in God who creates the conditions in which an emerging whole develops, where complex and 'beautiful co-adaptedness among organic life forms' are seen; this is not just driven by a 'blind will to power' (see Ward in **TAYLOR**).

IRREDUCIBLE COMPLEXITY AND INTELLIGENT DESIGN

A relatively recent development, advocated by scientists such as BEHE and **PERCIVAL DAVIS**, has sought to challenge the premise of evolution that small and accidental mutations explain how a species continues to survive. The idea of **IRREDUCIBLE COMPLEXITY** states that some systems in nature are so dependent on all parts of the system developing together that without any one of those parts the whole system would break down.

The most cited example **BEHE** provided was that of the **FLAGELLUM**, which is a tail-like appendage that propels certain bacterium. The three known varieties of the flagellum each require the interaction of many (40) 'parts', which, Behe has argued, could not function as a whole under the evolutionary model where small changes occur independently to the separate parts. In Behe's own words,

> *'By irreducibly complex I mean a single system composed of several well-matched, interacting parts that contribute to the basic function, wherein the removal of any one of the parts causes the system to effectively cease functioning'.*

The evidence of irreducibly complex organisms is part of a position known as **INTELLIGENT DESIGN** (ID). This holds that, 'certain features of the universe and of living things are best explained by an intelligent cause, not an undirected process such as natural selection.' With links to **PALEY**'S design argument, proponents of ID have drawn attention to the complexity of DNA, with its precise ordering, as well as the 'sequence of protease reactions involving enzymes' (**DEWAR**) that enables blood to clot, as evidence that certain processes are irreducibly complex and not only challenge Darwinian evolution but suggest an intelligent designer. To stress:

> *'Intelligent design theorists argue that while some systems and organs can be explained by evolution, those that are irreducibly complex cannot, but instead an intelligent designer must be responsible.'*

RESPONSES TO IRREDUCIBLE COMPLEXITY AND INTELLIGENT DESIGN

Irreducible Complexity has presumed that a part of a system has always been part of that system. As **LACEWING** notes, however, the evolutionary process may have 'co-opted' parts into doing something else, and these parts which work in the tail of the flagellum, 'had nothing at all to do with movement when they first evolved; they could have evolved as a pump, and later on some further accidental change meant they joined with some new part to move a tail.' **DUNKLEBERG** goes through Behe's argument in great detail noting that the bacterial flagella have several functions and can evolve more abilities.

It is difficult to know when the term '**IRREDUCIBLE COMPLEXITY**' applies; it is scientists that have labelled things as 'parts' and not nature itself that neatly operates under these terms. Where does a system end? Again, medical practitioners may decide this, but once one thinks of the digestive system then one could include saliva and chewing, the lower intestine, stomach acids etc. Is there a 'closed system' in which IC can be said to work? As **DUNKLEBERG** notes,

> *'Evolution doesn't even notice whether a combination of parts, system and function chosen by an observer happens to satisfy a definition in a book. It just doesn't matter.'*

Dunkleberg notes further that if **IRREDUCIBLE COMPLEXITY** is proof of **INTELLIGENT DESIGN** and the example given of IC to prove ID is the flagellum bacterium, then 'this has the unintended consequence of making The Designer (God) responsible for serious diseases', such as diarrhoea, which kills thousands of infants each year, and the Bubonic Plague. This links back to arguments against God being a good designer of the universe studied in the **TELEOLOGICAL ARGUMENT**.

STRENGTHS AND WEAKNESSES

- In every other chapter in this guide a strength and weakness section has been included. However the science/religion debate is so multi-faceted that it is difficult to do such and so this chapter has explored arguments for and against each position as they have been presented. However, further areas of exploration might be:

- Is it feasible for **DAWKINS** to take a position which seems to be as **DOGMATIC** as those he opposes? Is this good science? **POPPER'S FALSIFICATION METHOD** would suggest that all scientific findings are provisional and cautious. As **WILKINSON** and **CAMPBELL** note, there have been reactions to Dawkins from within the scientific community. Dawkins may have mistakenly assumed that those within a faith tradition are putting forward a God as an alternative scientific explanation. Dawkins might reply that creationists and those who support intelligent design are doing precisely that, but creationism is not the only position that Christians take when interpreting the Genesis accounts, and it is questionable if Dawkins pays due consideration to other Christian positions.

- To what extent can either religion or science say with **ABSOLUTE CERTAINTY** that there is or isn't an ultimate explanation for the universe? How would we arrive at such a conclusion? Are there limits here to what can be said?

KEY QUOTES

1. *'While it is undoubtedly true that science is based on empirical methods, science does not disprove the existence of God. Instead, science such as cosmology helps us to better understand the universe in which we live'. Taylor, who goes on to quote McGrath and McGrath:*

2. *'One of the greatest disservices that Dawkins has done to the natural sciences is to portray them as relentlessly and inexorably atheistic. They are nothing of the sort'.*

3. *'The cold rational universe we have been offered during the age of science, its minutest details docketed and documented, and its reduction of man to one outgrowth among many of chemistry, physics and biology, seems to exclude all that is more intense, thrilling, moving and perplexing in human experience'..... 'The closer we get to the heart of reality the more we encounter the paradoxical and the inexplicable. The truest vision of the universe leads us out of science, and indeed beyond rational thought and language'. Harriott in Richards*

4. *'There is no spirit-driven life force, no throbbing, heaving, pullulating, protoplasmic, mystic jelly. Life is just bytes and bytes of digital information'. Dawkins*

5. 'It is important to point out that if religion cannot claim to have a monopoly of truth, neither can science. It is one thing to have a rule that: 'What is proved should be accepted', but quite another to have a rule that: Only what is proved should be accepted'. Such a rule cannot itself be proved!' Richards

6. 'Science is not neutral, it does not just deal with facts. The possibilities opened up by science [such as cures to illnesses that were previously seen as a punishment from the Gods or fate] automatically feed into people's expectations and understandings of life'. Thompson

7. 'The fundamentalists deny that evolution has taken place; they deny that the earth and the universe as a whole are more than a few thousand years old, and so on. There is ample scientific evidence that the fundamentalists are wrong in these matters, and that their notions of cosmogony have about as much basis in fact as the Tooth Fairy has'. Asimov

8. 'We are not now looking to the physical world for hints of God's existence but to God's existence as an aid for understanding why things have developed in the physical world in the manner that they have.' Polkinghorne in Jordan et al

9. 'Evolution does not require the nonexistence of God, it merely

allows for it. That alone is enough to evoke condemnation from those who fear the nonexistence of God more than they fear God Himself'. Doyle

10. 'Darwin's theories showed: 'a tendency to limit God's glory in creation', that 'the principle of natural selection is absolutely incompatible with the word of God', and that 'it contradicts the revealed relations of creation to its Creator.'' An article by Wilberforce quoted in Ahluwalia

11. 'The theory of evolution by cumulative natural selection is the only theory we know of that is in principle capable of explaining the existence of organized complexity'. Dawkins

CONFUSIONS TO AVOID

Creationism is a relatively modern-day belief. **WARD** has said that it will be a fruitless search to find a mainstream theologian who believed in a literal reading of Genesis before the 18th Century. **PHILO**, a 1st Century Jewish philosopher, noted that where Genesis 1 and 2 seemed to clash, mythological interpretations were always favourable as they got to the deeper meaning of the text. This kind of view was influential upon Christian interpretation of the **TORAH**. Note: if you said that Christians have always read the Genesis account literally, that would be inaccurate. Many Christians read the Genesis account as a myth, meaning it has deeper teaching than can be gained from a literal reading.

If evolution is attacked because it is only a 'theory' this shows a lack of understanding of how the term theory is used in science. **TAYLOR** notes that, 'in science, a theory refers to an established explanation of and account of some feature of the physical world that has been established by scientific research, supported by scientific laws.' Many who use the term theory in a derogatory manner actually mean that evolution is an unproven **HYPOTHESIS**, but it is actually regarded with more weight than that in science due to the evidence it produces to support its theory.

Be careful when referring to interesting points in history such as the debate between Huxley and Wilberforce and the **SCOPES** trial. These should be **ILLUSTRATIVE** rather than given in detail. Be careful also to try to present the key points of the positions on each side of the creationist/evolution debate. Much of the current rhetoric about these issues, which concern worldviews rather than just obscure and unimportant beliefs, has been heated and marked by stereotyping which fails to hear what those who hold different views are stating. Having said that, it is felt strongly by **DAWKINS** that creationist beliefs are not just harmless, but dangerous, anti-scientific and ignorant.

Exam Rescue Remedy

1. Build your own scaffolding which represents the logic of the theory. Use a mind map or a summary sheet.

2. Do an analysis of past questions by theme as well as by year (see philosophicalinvestigations.co.uk website for examples). Try writing your own Philosophy of Religion paper based on what hasn't come up recently.

3. Examine examiners' reports (go to their website) for clues as to how to answer a question well.

4. Use the **AREA** approach suggested in this revision guide. **ARGUMENT**- Have I explained the argument (from Plato or Kant for example)? **RESPONSE** - Have I outlined and explained a good range of responses to the argument? **EVALUATION** - Now I have clearly set out positions, what do I think of these? Is mine **A PHILOSOPHICAL** argument and why. Does the original argument stand or fall against the criticisms raised? Why or why not?

5. List relevant technical vocabulary for inclusion in essay (eg efficient cause, form of the good, analytic, synthetic).

6. Prepare key quotes from selected key authors, original/ contemporary (eg quotes list from the A level website philosophicalinvestigations.co.uk – even better, produce your own). Learn some.

7. Contrast and then evaluate different views/theories/authors as

some questions ask "which approach is best?" So contrast every approach with one other and decide beforehand what you think.

8. Practise writing for 35 minutes. Don't use a computer, unless you do so in the exam.

9. Always answer and discuss the exact question in front of you, never learn a "model answer". Use your own examples (newspapers, films, documentaries, real life). Be prepared to think creatively and adapt your knowledge to the question.

10. Conclude with your view, justify it (give reasons) especially with "discuss".

Bibliography

- **AHLUWALIA, L** - Understanding Philosophy of Religion OCR, Folens, 2008

- **BARON, P** - Religious Studies (AS Ethics), Inducit Learning, 2011

- **BOWIE, R** - AS/A2 Philosophy of Religion and Religious Ethics for OCR, Nelson Thornes, 2004

- **COLE, P** - Access to Philosophy: Philosophy of Religion, Hodder & Stoughton, 2005

- **DEWAR, G** - Oxford Revision Guides: AS & A Level Religious Studies: Philosophy and Ethics Through Diagrams, Oxford University Press, 2009

- **JACKSON, R** - The God of Philosophy, The Philosophers' Magazine, 2001

- **JORDAN, A** - Lockyer., N Tate, E., Philosophy of Religion for A Level OCR Edition, Nelson Thornes, 2004

- **LACEWING, M** - Philosophy for AS, Routledge, 2008

- **PHELAN, JW** - Philosophy Themes and Thinkers, Cambridge University Press, 2005

- **RICHARDS, HJ** - Philosophy of Religion, Heinemann, 2004

- **RUSSELL, B** - History of Western Philosophy, Routledge

Classics, 1946 (2008).

- **TAYLOR, I, EYRA, C, KNIGHT, R** - OCR Religious Studies Philosophy and Ethics AS, Heinemann, 2008

- **TAYLOR, M** - OCR Philosophy of Religion for AS and A2, Routledge, 2009

- **THOMPSON, M** - An Introduction to Philosophy and Ethics, Hodder & Stoughton, 2009

- **WILKINSON, M & CAMPBELL, H** - Philosophy of Religion for AS Level, Continuum, 2009

Electronic Resources

- http://www.big-bang-theory.com

- http://www.ccel.org/ccel/schaff/npnf102.iv.XII.7.html

- http://www.ccel.org/ccel/schaff/npnf103.iv.ii.xiii.html

- http://www.darwinproject.ac.uk/entry-2814

- http://josephkenny.joyeurs.com/CDtexts/summa/index.html

- http://journals.cambridge.org/abstract_S0034412509990369

- http://www.jstor.org/discover/10.2307/3327630?
  uid=2&uid=4&sid=21101136290147

- http://nwcreation.net/intelligentdesign.html

- http://www.newscientist.com/blogs/nstv/2011/07/how-the-universe-
  appeared-from-nothing.html

- www.philosophicalinvestigations.co.uk

- http://www.philosophypathways.com/newsletter/issue119.html

- http://www.talkorigins.org/faqs/behe.html

Postscript

Brian Poxon is Head of Religious Studies at Wells Cathedral School in Somerset. He gained a first class honours degree in Theology and Religious Studies, and a Masters in Holocaust Theology at Bristol University. Brian went on to teach Religious Studies in a large comprehensive school in South Gloucestershire.

In 2003, Brian was appointed as Head of Religious Education at Bristol Cathedral School, which proved to be ideal preparation for establishing a Religion, Philosophy and Ethics department at Ballarat Grammar School, Australia from 2008-2012. Whilst in Australia Brian helped to establish the successful nationwide Philosothon event.

In 2007 a philosophy and ethics community was established dedicated to enlarging the teaching of philosophy in schools by applying the theory of multiple intelligences to the analysis of philosophical and ethical problems. To join the community please register your interest by filling in your details on the form on the website. We welcome contributions and suggestions so that our community continues to flourish and expand.

www.philosophicalinvestigations.co.uk

All quotes from Aquinas are from Summa Theologicae: josephkenny.joyeurs.com